To **Jan Carla** –

the light of my life and love of my heart

THE JESUS MODEL

Planting Churches the Jesus Way

DIETRICH SCHINDLER

First published in English in Great Britain by Piquant Editions in 2013. Piquant Editions is an imprint of Piquant.

Piquant: PO Box 83, Carlisle, CA3 9GR, UK

www.piquanteditions.com

ISBN-13 for Print: 978-1-909281-23-3
Related ISBN for Epub: 978-1-909281-24-0
Related ISBN for Mobi/Kindle: 978-1-909281-25-7

A catalogue record for this publication is available from the British Library.

Originally published in German as *Das Jesus-Modell: Gemeinden gründen wie Jesus* (Witten: SCM R. Brockhaus, 2010) ISBN 978-3-417-26343-5

Note: Except for personalities known to the general public and for members of the author's own family, the names of people have been changed in order to preserve their confidentiality.

Cover design by Luz Design, projectluz.com

Contents

LIST OF FIGURES

Acknowledgements

'You can't fill your sails with wind you make yourself'

– Karl Heinrich Waggerl (Austrian writer, 1897–1973)

For the wind in my sails and in the sails of this book, I am indebted to a number of people who were at my side with assistance. First of all I thank my dear wife Jan Carla and our three children, Erich (and his wife Kelley), Monica, and Lukas. Time and again you encouraged me, and thus helped me to finish this project well. Much of what I have discovered in Jesus, I see in you, too. I also owe heartfelt thanks to my beloved mother, Thea Schindler, who constantly encouraged me through her prayers.

Further, I'd like to thank a number of people who are much better writers than I am, and who helped improve my manuscript. Special thanks go to Beate Tumat, Artur Schmitt, Heinz Weickel, Reinhard Spincke, Prof. Craig Ott, Carsten Finger, Kenneth Yoder, Martin Plücker, Julia Teschke, and Silke Geiss for their contributions. I'm also thankful to the Program Leader at SCM R. Brockhaus Publishing Company, Hans-Werner Durau and to Tom Keefer who translated the book from German into English. Special thanks go to Elria Kwant for her tireless work to make this English edition shine.

These encouragers are the wind in the sails of this book. Sole responsibility for the contents, however, remains mine.

Dietrich Schindler

Foreword by Martin Robinson

It is not uncommon for people to use Jesus as a model for leadership training, discipleship development, prayer or many other aspects of the Christian life, but I have never previously thought about Jesus as providing a model for church planting. That could be a shortcoming on my part, so I am indebted to Dietrich for provoking my thought in this area.

It's reasonable to be a little sceptical when someone suggests a 'Jesus model' for anything. It can easily be the case that we have a preformed model in mind that we then seek to validate through references to Jesus. But I think Dietrich has understood some of the deeper foundations that allow church planting to be much more than a formula, or worse still, merely a marketing operation.

His starting point, namely that church planters are stronger in the area of action than they are in that of reflection, is consistent with my experience and I am impressed with the depth of reflection that he has engaged in. His practical experience means that his theoretical constructs ring true. Dietrich offers the church planter some genuine reflective practice.

Towards the end of the book, Dietrich tackles the two subjects that church planters often avoid, and yet these are precisely the issues that can transform a single valiant effort at church planting into a genuine movement. 'Discipleship' and 'Empowering Leadership' are the two areas that church planters – anxious to move quickly to the next task – often avoid, but it's impossible to build replicating structures and movements without significant investment in these areas.

This is a book that can only be written the other side of many mistakes, extensive experience of planting and a highly honest examination of the questions to be faced. These insights are ones to be anticipated with the same delight that one might approach a gourmet meal. Enjoy your reading, but don't rush through any page, savour the contents and digest them slowly.

Martin Robinson is the author of several books, including *Winning Hearts, Changing Minds* (2001) and *Planting Mission-Shaped Churches Today* (2006). He is the national Director of 'Together in Mission', a trans-denominational para-church organization, and the Principal of Springdale College, UK. Dr Robinson worked as a church planter in Birmingham and in leadership training with the Bible Society.

Introduction

Church planters are a rare breed of people. They're restless. It bothers them that people around them are living without Jesus and are unaware that they are lost. They can't bear it, and they won't have it. It's totally unacceptable. It ought not to be!

Church planters exhibit particular characteristics. They are visionaries who see a future that most people don't see – a future the way God wants it to be. They are full of faith – able to trust God, and able to thank him in advance for the people who are going to find Christ. They are goal oriented and persistent – they know what they want and are not easily deterred. They are praying people who love to spend time with God praying for people and events. They are people-oriented – able to make new contacts, build relationships and cultivate friendships. They are hard workers who roll up their sleeves and are not afraid to get their hands dirty, who don't shy away from menial tasks.

Because they're restless, church planters tend to jump right in with both feet and get moving toward the goal. They take initiative. Often they're impatient. You could say that they follow their gut. They are likely to act first, and only afterwards decide whether their course of action was wise. Church planters want to make progress and create change. What counts for them, is results: the world needs new churches!

The ultimate model for every church planter is – how could it be otherwise? – the Apostle Paul. Paul was always on the go, hard working and successful. Every church planter wants to be like him, to follow his example and see the same results: the good news of Jesus as Saviour and Lord spread throughout the world, people's hearts touched, their lives changed and new churches established. Just as the Apostle Paul did in the first century, church planters today want to get to work and see results. I know what I'm talking about, because I belong to this rare breed of people.

Ever since I was 20 years old, I have harboured a unique longing in my heart, which I constantly brought before God, asking him to grant me his favour. With his help I wanted to plant five churches in Germany in my lifetime. 'Five to grow before I go' became my life motto. Eighteen years later, this dream has become a reality. My wife and I, along with our three children, have had the privilege of seeing much fruit over the past twenty-three years. People came to faith in Christ, churches were planted, believers were trained, leaders empowered. I made plenty of mistakes along the way – mistakes that caused pain for others as well as for myself. I've learned a lot about how to plant churches, and about how not to plant churches.

I've learned that one of the greatest strengths that church planters tend to possess – that 'get-it-done' attitude – can also be one of their greatest weaknesses. That's why I've written this book. When a sailboat is built, it's given a keel with ballast so that it won't overturn and sink, even during a storm at sea. Ballast is what gives the sailing vessel stability and security, especially when high winds and high seas threaten. The purpose of this book is to give church planters the ballast they need. It's what lies beneath the surface that determines success or failure in church planting, not the things that are visible above the surface. It's not the church-planting methods but rather the character of the church planter and the way he or she goes about the work that makes the difference.

But what would a sailboat be without sails? Probably just a somewhat better raft. That's why this book seeks to unlock principles for church planters from the life of Jesus, and to make those principles practical and applicable to ministry today. In addition, attention will be given to the special challenges that occur during the start-up phase, as well as those that occur during later stages.

This book will help tomorrow's church planters rediscover how Jesus can be their example, their motivation, their ballast, indeed their very reason for being in the business of church planting. When we look for principles and practical steps for church planting, we'll find them in the life and ministry of Jesus.

Who will benefit from this book? Young church planters without much experience, certainly, but also for more experienced church planters there is solid, practical advice and a fresh perspective here. Seminary and Bible school students, as well as leadership teams of established churches can gain instruction for taking action as well as tips for avoiding obstacles and meeting challenges with God's help. And individual Christians who feel called to be part of a church-planting team will find a solid foundation for their calling here. My own experience was gained in the Evangelical Free Church in Germany. The principles I outline, however, should be adaptable to most denominational structures.

All those who want to plant churches in our postmodern world are likely to find that they are in for the greatest adventure of their lives, inevitably with highs and lows. Such adventurers will find that they need the best equipment, the most reliable guides, the most nourishing food, alert eyes and, most of all, the favour of the living God. May this book deliver just what church planters need today.

The following prayer, spoken in the quietness of your heart, may just be your first step on a brand-new journey into the adventure of church planting:

Lord Jesus Christ,

Thank you that you made me as I am. I also want to become like you in your devotion to the Father and in your passionate love for people. And so I open my heart to you and say, 'May your kingdom come, your will be done on earth, and in my life, as it is in heaven.' And may this happen in me and through me for your glory. Amen.

PART I

THE JESUS MODEL:

Principles for Church Planting from the Life of Jesus

ONE

Jesus as 'Church Planter'

'Your first ministry assignment is your second degree.' That's what I generally say to young people who are just getting started in church ministry. I especially like to remind them of this if they have already experienced disappointments or setbacks in the ministry. The truth is, sometimes *we* shape the people we are ministering to. More often it's those people and the ministry itself that shapes us. The early years of ministry are often rich with experiences that help us grow in self-awareness.

But before we earn our 'second degree', we need to complete our first degree by studying church planting and church growth. I studied theology at Trinity Evangelical Divinity School in Deerfield, Illinois (a Chicago suburb) and was fortunate enough to receive this training from a professor who was an experienced church planter. David Hesselgrave was a former missionary who had planted churches in Japan; he had also already written one of the first books on church planting. In this foundational work, *Planting Churches Cross-Culturally*, Hesselgrave describes what he calls the 'Pauline Cycle' of church planting. Using the book of Acts as a guide, Hesselgrave outlines the steps that Paul and his co-workers took to establish new churches – steps that are not chronological but rather systematic. Because I realized I needed a systematic approach if I were to be successful, I wrote, and later implemented, my own plan for planting churches based on the steps of Hesselgrave's Pauline Cycle.

Over the years, church-planting methodology is a subject that I've thought much about, read much about, experimented with and put into practice. I realized that in almost all the relevant literature, including Hesselgrave's works, the emphasis is on the Apostle Paul. Most books and articles describe what Paul did during his missionary journeys, and how we can use a similar approach today. Without question we can indeed learn a great deal about church planting and church growth from Paul. One day, however, I began to think about Jesus and church planting. Was Paul really the first missionary and church planter, or was there someone before him? I began to read the Gospels with new eyes, asking myself questions about Jesus and church planting. I was amazed how many principles Jesus embodied that were later applied by Paul. Could it be that Jesus was the first missionary and the first church planter, and that Paul and his co-workers, led by the Holy Spirit, learned from Jesus' example?

This book contains the results of my research – the 'Jesus Model' of church planting and church growth. It's from Jesus that we discover that God seeks and finds his way into the lives of men and women, draws them to himself, and builds his kingdom. I can't imagine anything more exciting or more worthwhile than learning from Jesus how to plant a church.

Where do we begin? We begin with longing. My parents came from Germany and settled in Wisconsin (USA). My mother came from a family of refugees who, because of the war, had to leave behind everything they owned in Silesia (then northeastern Germany, now part of Poland). For nine long months they travelled by foot. Their lives were in danger. They suffered from malnourishment and extreme duress. When they finally arrived in my grandfather's hometown near Offenburg in the Black Forest (in southwestern Germany, near France and Switzerland), they tried to build a new life. It was in Offenburg that my mother and father met and fell in love. Six months after they married, they emigrated, against the wishes of their parents, to the United States. For the second time in her young life, my mother had to leave behind her home.

My parents arrived in Milwaukee, where I was born. It was a city filled with German immigrants and known for its beer. Here they sought to build a new life. But instead of upward mobility and a better standard of living, my parents experienced new setbacks and difficulties. Although my father had training and skills as both an electrician and a tool-and-die-maker, he was unable to find work. And although he wasn't an American citizen, he received a draft notice from the army. Following the advice of an American friend, he enlisted in the navy. As a result, this young couple had to move to a distant city on the East Coast, and for the next two years my father was at sea. As you might imagine, my mother suffered enormous homesickness. She was in a strange city, without her husband, with no friends, no family, no church, no money, skant provisions and only a limited knowledge of the English language. If there had been a bridge between North America and Europe, my mother would have gladly walked across the Atlantic to get 'home'. That's the incredible power of longing.

'A strong desire, a craving, *especially* for something seemingly unattainable' is how *longing* can be defined. Other definitions include the element of an inner desire so intense as to be painful. That would certainly have applied to my mother. But Jesus, too, experienced this deep longing. He had a desire that was so strong that he was willing to endure pain, rejection, shame, violence – the worst this world had to give – in order to see his desire fulfilled. What could have caused Jesus to leave the joy of undiluted fellowship with God the Father and God the Holy Spirit but a profound, persistent and deep longing?

Jesus' Longing

Jesus' longing led him to an ill-reeking garbage dump outside the city of Jerusalem two thousand years ago. His passion to free people from their guilt and their alienation from God led him to the Holy Week – and to suffering and death. Jesus died so that guilty sinners could stand justified before God at his expense. Jesus died so that we can be totally renewed, 'born again'. Jesus died so that his love could be tangible and accessible to us. Jesus died so that we might take part in his new world. Jesus died so that we could become God's adopted children and look him in the eyes without fear or shame. Jesus died to establish a new society, with a new community called 'the church'.

Jesus gave voice to his longing when he said: 'I will build my church, and the gates of Hades will not overcome it' (Matthew 16:18). That's both a mission statement and a declaration of love. The incarnation, the life and teaching of Jesus, his death and resurrection – all of it was focussed on this one goal: the church. Jesus wants to build his church, purify her, strengthen her, liberate her, empower her, multiply her. His heart burns with love for his church. She embodies his great passion and longing. He'll give everything for her. Because the church originates with Jesus, the church is the hope of the world. If Christians love what Jesus loves, then they will love the church. In the final analysis, ecclesiology (the doctrine of the church) and Christology (the doctrine of Christ) are intimately connected, and ecclesiology arises out of missiology (the doctrine of missions).

Jesus thinks highly of the church. What about you? Do you think highly of the church? Of your church – what she is like now, and what she can become? Are your church and your involvement in it:

- a privilege and not a burden?
- a joy and not a curse?
- an experience of safety and acceptance?
- full of grace and forgiveness?
- a source of life change, based on God's strength?
- a 'maternity ward' where people far from God are born again and become God's children?

Anyone who wants to plant churches must be excited about the church. We find many images in the Bible that express excitement and amazement about the church. The church is a bride, embraced by the love and care of Jesus (Ephesians 5:25–33). The church is a spiritual body, complete with all the character traits of God himself (Ephesians 1:23). The church is a branch, heavy with juice-filled grapes that draw their power from Christ, who is the vine (John 15:1). The church is a place of intimate fellowship and undisturbed community with God (Ephesians 2:19; 1 John 1:5–7). The church has meaning and direction in a world that's dark, lost and confused. The church is God's buffer against the devices of hell. The church that God envisions is everything we ever dared to dream of.

The church is a family that has sworn allegiance to Christ, a family that's faithful to him and to one another, a family whose life is from him and for him, a family who makes him known to a world of lost, lonely, longing people. Wherever his family gives witness to his love by their lives and by their words, strangers become friends. They become part of God's new community. As new members of his family, they in turn love others – encourage, support, liberate them – so that these, in turn, can love and support still others. That's how the church grows, in both quality and quantity. And it includes the multiplication of churches through planting new congregations.

Church Planting Starts with Jesus

It has to, because 'church' was Jesus' idea in the first place. He's the one who gave birth to the church. That's why church planting begins with Jesus. It doesn't start with people or methods or goals. It starts with Jesus. It's true that Jesus blesses people and methods and goals. They have their rightful place, but only after he has been given *his* rightful place by the church.

In emphasizing the role of Jesus in church planting, we are not in any way minimizing the role of the Father and the Holy Spirit. It goes without saying that both the Father and the Spirit are as fully involved in the birth and growth of a church as Jesus is. Church planting and church growth have a Trinitarian foundation.[1] Nevertheless it's Jesus, the second Person of the Trinity, who came into this world to 'give God a face'. It's through him that we know the Father and the Spirit in a personal way.

I derive my ideas about church planting from the vision of a church that is living close to the heart of Jesus, living out Jesus' dream for the church. What do I mean when I talk about church planting? Church planting is the *extension* of unclouded fellowship with God in Christ, which is intentionally sought by a committed *leadership,* who *connects* lost people with Christ and Christians, flowing into the *harvest,* resulting in *new churches* planted.

This definition needs further clarification. First of all, 'the *continuation* of an unclouded fellowship with God in Christ' means church planting has its origins in the relational intimacy among the persons of the Trinity. When Jesus commanded us to baptize disciples in the name of the Father, the Son and the Holy Spirit, he wasn't dictating a formula for us to repeat at baptisms. Baptism is an outward expression of the inner reality that a disciple has been immersed into fellowship with the Trinity. Church planters actively extend this experience of unclouded fellowship with God.

Church planting arises from a 'committed *leadership*' with a deep longing. Because Jesus wants to see new churches started, he looks for

---

1 See Reimer, Ch 4.1, "Trinitarische Grundkonzeption", pp 130–49.

people who are risk-takers, people who are influencers. We call them leaders. A leader is a disciple of Jesus Christ who can influence other people for Christ's purposes. Churches aren't started by accident; they are started intentionally by people who submit themselves gladly to taking risks for Jesus' sake because of their deep longing to be used by God.

Church planting *connects* lost people to Christ. The connecting links are Christians, because they live in two worlds. Church planting will always have Jesus' goal in mind, to seek and to save the lost (Luke 19:10). Jesus called that disciple-making, and his followers are called to make disciples of all the nations. Discipleship doesn't begin with conversion. It starts *before* conversion. Conversions happen because discipleship has already been in action. Newly converted Christ-followers learn to live as Jesus lived: in the joy of the Lord with others, and from the resources God provides.

Church planting yields a *harvest*. The harvest is the goal, Jesus reminded us (Matthew 9:35–38), which determines the entire direction of the ministry. It's not about the barn; it's about the harvest. That's why a newly planted church will want to plant other new churches and will spend itself to achieve that.

The gospel – the proclamation of Jesus Christ as Saviour from sin and guilt and as a guideline for living – is the central message of the church and the pathway to new churches. Christ-centred churches are gospel-centred churches. To accept the gospel is to be set *free*. In John's Gospel, Jesus taught the people how his crucifixion would verify the gospel (John 8:21–29). Those who believe in Jesus will follow him and obey him. The result for them is freedom from sin and freedom to live as Christ prompts them to live. So the gospel has a liberating effect – it frees us from ourselves and frees us for Christ.

How do we know when a church has been successfully planted? We know it when we witness the gospel being proclaimed, people turning to Christ and accepting his work on the cross for the forgiveness of their sin, following his lordship, growing in their faith, living in a fellowship of commitment and service with other Christians, and when leaders have been identified.

Jesus as 'Church Planter'

People entering a profession or trade today must be ready to be flexible throughout the course of their careers. Jesus' calling demands a similar flexibility. In order to offer people salvation from sin and to bring them into fellowship with God the Father, Jesus had to assume a number of very different, yet complementary, roles.

Jesus said that he was sent by the Father. Thus we may say that Jesus was a missionary. Missionaries are people who are called by God to leave their own culture, to immerse themselves in a different culture, so that people far from God in that culture can come to know him personally. Another word for 'sent one' or 'missionary' is the term 'apostle'. Apostles are people sent by God, under his authority, invested with his power, to represent him and to do his work. The early Christians saw Jesus in this light, as an apostle (Hebrews 3:1).

The Gospel of John is a treasure trove of references to Jesus and his awareness of his role as missionary. John's Gospel refers to Jesus as 'sent one' or 'one sent from God' more than 40 times. Jesus was God, yet he left behind the fellowship with the Father and the Holy Spirit to come into this world, which he himself had created (John 1:10–11). He made his home with us. He lived among us (in Greek literally, he 'pitched his tent among us', in John 1:14). 'God did not send his Son into the world to condemn the world, but to save the world through him' (John 3:17). Jesus thought of himself as someone who was sent by God to do God's work (John 7:29). So it's not surprising that Jesus sent his disciples into the world with the same assignment he had received from his Father (John 17:18).

Jesus was not only a missionary. He was also a sovereign king. It's true that he went around incognito, and people didn't recognize him as king. Yet it's quite clear that he knew himself to be a king. Pilate heard from Jesus' own lips that he was indeed a king, but that his kingdom was not of this world (John 18:36). The kingdom of God appeared in this world in the person of Jesus (Luke 17:21). A king is the richest person in his kingdom, and the most powerful. What the king wants, the king gets. All of the king's subjects live by his favour. When people give themselves to Christ, they submit to his lordship. To have Jesus as Saviour is to have him as king. That's why Jesus' disciples follow the instructions of their king. They know he's always in the right.

People sometimes find it hard to believe in Jesus because he spoke so simply. The most profound things in life are often the easiest to understand, yet the most difficult to put into practice. That's true of Jesus' claim to be king.

When it comes right down to it, there are only two possibilities in our world: I can build *my* kingdom, or I can build *God's* kingdom. Some people come to Christ and say, 'Jesus, I want you in my life', but what they mean is that they're at the end of their rope. They want to be free from the weight of their guilt, and they're desperate. They realize that they can't cope with the demands of life on their own. They want Jesus in their life, so that Jesus can help *them* to fulfil *their* plans. But Jesus isn't interested in that. It's much too small a goal for him, too meaningless, too 'earth-un-shaking'. That's why Jesus invites us to become citizens of God's kingdom, where Jesus is king, where his word rules, where he has the last word. That's the meaning of what we ask for when we pray, 'Your kingdom come, your will be done, on earth (and in my life) as it is in heaven.' The idea is not for us to invite Jesus into *our* lives and *our* plans, but for us to be invited into *his* life and *his* plans, so that we become part of the building of *his* kingdom.

Jesus is a missionary, a 'sent one', an apostle, a king. And Jesus is also a church planter. What proof do I have for that? We must see Jesus as a church planter because he saw himself in that way. He said, 'I will build my church' (Matthew 16:18). This clearly shows that church planting and church growth is Jesus' intentional goal, and that he himself will accomplish this goal. Some may argue that Jesus, in the quoted context, was speaking to Peter, and that it was Peter who would build the church. But Jesus uses the first person pronoun: '*I* will build my church.' Jesus sees himself as the builder and architect, and Peter as his workman under his command.

Luke, another Christ-follower who wrote the book of Acts, understood Jesus in just this way. Luke introduced his history of the early church by saying that his previous book (the Gospel of Luke) was a report of 'all that Jesus *began* to do and to teach' (Acts 1:1). The beginnings were the foundation that Luke had written about in his Gospel. After the *beginning* comes the *continuation* in the life of the early church. And what do we read there? We read that Jesus' disciples called people to turn from their sin and turn to Jesus. The evangelistic preaching and teaching of the early church led to the establishment of many churches, because the result of evangelism is either that new believers are assimilated into existing churches or that new churches are planted. The book of Acts is a testimony to the activity of Jesus as church planter, at work through his disciples.

Indeed, church planting was so much a part of the life of the early church that we read an amazing statement: 'So the churches were strengthened in the faith and grew daily in numbers' (Acts 16:5). This is a breath-taking assessment that is far too often simply overlooked. Many readers think that the number of *believers* grew daily. That's true, of course, but it's not what this statement means. Here Luke tells us that the number of *churches* grew daily.[2] And these new churches were the work of Jesus, the church planter.

The book of Acts is the *continuation* of the ministry of Jesus on earth through the activity of his disciples. Working in partnership with Jesus, they planted churches. But how did they know how to go about this work? Quite simply, they saw and heard and learned from Jesus himself. Jesus was their model. He had put it into practice among them: the disciples were his first church. In order to change the entire world, Jesus invested the last three years of his life in a team of twelve people. The Gospels show us Jesus in his 'career' as church planter. His life teaches us both the principles and the practice we need in order to plant churches ourselves, working in partnership with him.

In conclusion: Church planting starts with Jesus and leads to Jesus. The church is Jesus' great longing. He continues to plant churches through men and women who are devoted to him and who live his life in a world far from God.

The word 'radical' comes from the Latin *radix*, which means 'source, root, foundation'. Church planting arises from its root, Jesus, and as such, church planting is truly *radical*.

---

2 The grammar of this verse in the original leaves no doubt that "the churches" increased in numbers daily, and not, as often thought, the number of disciples. Most commentators seem to have missed this. Schneider, in his exposition of this verse, says Luke always uses the Greek word *arithmo* (number) in connection with persons. See Schneider, p 202. This does not contradict but affirms our thesis, since churches are made up of persons.

TWO

The 'Jesus Model': An Overview

Frank Lloyd Wright (1867–1959) became a world-renown architect because of his unique style, which drew strongly on the natural surroundings of the buildings he designed. His tireless creative energy produced over 1000 designs and 500 houses. His homes, with their flat roofs, wide gables and waterfalls, are legendary. Today many of them are worth millions. Before Wright was born, his mother Anna discovered the 'Froebel gifts' at an exhibition in Philadelphia. Froebel gifts were geometric shapes made of wood, created by Friedrich Froebel (1782–1852) as educational toys that he used to teach young children spatial concepts as part of his childhood education curriculum. It was Froebel who coined the term 'kindergarten'. In his thinking, Froebel wanted children to experience learning in a setting that was fun and wonderful for them – like paradise; a garden for children, a *kinder*garden.

While she was still pregnant, Anna decorated her child's room with pictures of world-famous buildings. Frank Lloyd Wright played with Froebel gifts and had only to look at the pictures hanging in his room to imagine what those little toy blocks could become. These geometric forms were so influential for Wright that toward the end of his life he said, 'The maple wood blocks are in my fingers to this day.'

From a model in the hands of a child arose homes – sleek, sensuous homes whose designs are still imitated and whose beauty is still admired. Wooden blocks served as models for what would later become reality. A model differs from its original: it is a limited or simplified representation of its original; it shares only some of the original's most relevant qualities; and the model is functional – it exists to help us understand key aspects of the more complicated or vast original.

The 'Jesus Model' is intended to help us understand how Jesus went about his work, so that we can follow key aspects of his example as we go about the work of planting new churches.

The life and teaching of Jesus show us how we can plant churches today. Jesus' call to discipleship is the call to learn from him, to live and to work in the same way he did. If we can envisage ourselves as called to be part of a learning community, we will be able to learn the essentials of church planting from Jesus himself. 'Take my yoke upon you and learn from me' (Matthew 11:29) is the call to integrate Jesus' teaching (his yoke) and his life into our lives, so that Jesus can fulfil his plans through us. Imitation is a form of 'modelling' behaviour.

The term 'example' or 'model' comes to us from the world of minting coins. There a model is a mold, an image or shape that is stamped onto large quantities of coins. Jesus as church planter is our model, who shapes the way we plant churches. His way of doing things should be recognizable in our way of doing things.

What does the Jesus Model look like?

It is based on eight principles, which are not to be understood or applied in a linear, sequential way, but rather in a cyclical, overlapping and complementary way. It may be helpful to imagine these eight principles as circling round a single core, which acts like the nucleus of an atom that holds all the particles around it together. Without the core, the principles are unconnected, lifeless and meaningless. The eight principles all find their origin in, and derive their essence from, the core.

It's telling that Jesus built the kingdom of God through the proclamation of the gospel. Throughout his life, Jesus talked about the kingdom of God and said that it was beginning in our world because he was present. Just before Jesus' public ministry began, John the Baptist announced the arrival of the kingdom: 'Repent, for the kingdom of heaven has come near ' (Matthew 3:2). When Jesus began his ministry in Galilee, he said, 'The time is fulfilled, and the kingdom of God has come near; repent, and believe in the good news' (Mark 1:15, NRSV, Anglicized; Matthew 4:17).

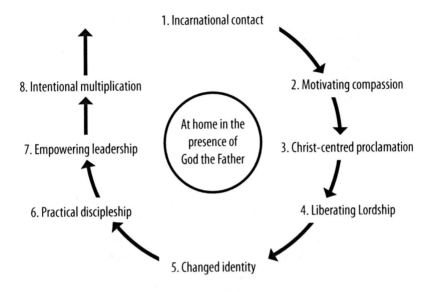

Figure 1: The 'Jesus Model' for planting churches

The coming of Jesus fulfilled the prophecy of Isaiah. In the 40 days after his resurrection, Jesus spoke of nothing else besides the one thing on his heart: the kingdom of God (Acts 1:3). The Apostles took the message of the kingdom so to heart that Paul, sitting in prison at the end of his life, proclaimed 'the kingdom of God' (Acts 28:31).

The kingdom of God is both the working of God in the hearts and the behaviour of his children as individuals, and the influence of God on a global scale, shaping geopolitical events in our world. The kingdom of God begins in the hearts of individuals and it spreads to families, churches and society as a whole. Especially when good overcomes evil, the kingdom of God becomes visible. The kingdom of God is where what God wants actually happens. It appears in the lives of his followers. They become a visible representation of the beauty of God, an object lesson for all to see, by allowing God to shape and colour their lives in any way he chooses. But what does the kingdom of God have to do with the planting of new churches?

Newly planted churches are a visible indication of the presence of the kingdom of God. In the church, it is neither education nor status nor wealth that matters, but rather the palpable influence of Jesus in the lives of his followers. Christians behave differently because Christ leads their lives. The church provides a glimpse of heaven and the world to come. What happens in heaven is reflected in the church when the name of God is held in awe, his will is done, his influence is felt and his life-giving joy is experienced: 'Church planting is thus the most urgent business of humankind. It is through the creation (or planting) of churches that God's kingdom is extended into communities which have not yet been touched by the precious surprise of the presence of the kingdom of God in their midst.'[1]

The kingdom of God spreads when new churches are established. In the church, Jesus shows himself as king. In the church, individuals experience a life change that the structures and systems of secular society are incapable of producing. Jesus Christ lives and leads in the church – he built his church in the first century, and he still builds his church today.

The Core: At Home in the Presence of God the Father

The crowds who flocked to Jesus were often so amazed that they couldn't stop talking about him. He had an appeal that was like nothing they had experienced before. 'They were astounded at his teaching, for he taught them as one having authority, and not [*like the boring teaching they were used to?*] as the scribes' (Mark 1:22, NRSV, Anglicized; cf. Mark 1:27). The thing that was so different about Jesus, the thing that drew people to him, was his authority.

Spiritual authority is a sign of strength that comes from being in the presence of God. Such authority can't be earned; it has to be granted by God. Jesus said, 'All authority in heaven and on earth has been given to me' (Matthew 28:18). Although authority cannot be earned, there is one condition to be fulfilled before God invests a person with authority: closeness to God the Father. Jesus constantly sought time alone in the presence of his Father. Intimacy with the Father was the fountain from which everything else in his life flowed.

---

1 Shenk & Stutzman, p 23.

Not long before his death on the cross and his departure from this world, Jesus taught his disciples about the Holy Spirit for the first time. This 'comforter' would be with them when Jesus was no longer present. Jesus called this gift of God 'another advocate' (John 14:16). The Holy Spirit is like Jesus, except that he is invisible and able to be present everywhere at the same time. Without the Holy Spirit, the disciples would not have been able to do the work Jesus gave them to do. They simply would not have had the authority, but Jesus' power, through the Holy Spirit, in the presence of the God the Father, bestowed authority.

Jesus was at home in the presence of his Father, and the Father was at home with Jesus. At Jesus' baptism, which marked the beginning of his public ministry, those present apparently heard the intimate words of God the Father: 'You are my Son, whom I love; with you I am well pleased' (Mark 1:11). Jesus often sought times and places where he could be alone with his Father and enjoy communion with him. 'In the morning, while it was still dark, he got up and went out to a deserted place, and there he prayed' (Mark 1:35, NRSV, Anglicized). After days of exhausting ministry, Jesus sought out his Father's company (see Mark 6:46; 9:7). Before the single greatest test he would ever face – his execution on the cross – he went to a grove of olive trees and prayed, '*Abba*, Father...' (Mark 14:35–36). *Abba* is an Aramaic term of endearment, a loving, intimate word for father, used by young children. Jesus breathed intimacy with his Father as we breathe oxygen. That intimacy was the source of his greatest joy and the strength behind everything he did.

This thirst for God, a deep longing, more intense than a baby's longing for its mother's milk, motivates the church planter. Jesus could never get enough of his Father. In the same way, an ever-present desire to be in the presence of the Father and in close fellowship with him must always be the starting point for a church planter. In the face of the greatest success or the worst defeat, a church planter finds deep contentment in the presence of God.

Principle 1: Incarnational Contact

Jesus' intimacy with God had a dramatic impact on his ministry. *Because* Jesus wanted to be close to his Father, he also wanted to be close to people.

This identifies Jesus as a church planter: Jesus was constantly on the go, wanting to be with people. The Catholic theologian Paul Michael Zulehner expressed it as 'submerging to be with God, re-surfacing to be with people'.[2]

Jesus went walking along the shores of the Sea of Galilee and met some fishermen (Mark 1:16). He visited new friends in their homes (Mark 1:29; Luke 10:38–39). He even spent time with the dregs of society – sinners and tax collectors (Mark 2:15). He wanted to be with people and he invited them to be with him (Mark 7:14). In one place we read that, 'Again crowds of people came to him' (Mark 10:1).

In many settings of his everyday life we see Jesus seeking contact with all sorts of people. We find him at a Jewish wedding (John 2:1–2), in conversation with a Samaritan woman of questionable morals (John 4), in a late-night discussion with a theologian (John 3), embracing children (Mark 10:16), helping the oppressed and healing the sick, at a social event in the home of a tax collector (Luke 5:29–32), moving among the grieving guests at a funeral (Luke 7:11–15), and in the company of a Roman army officer (Matthew 8:5–13). Why is it that Jesus travelled through so many towns and villages? Because he was looking for *people*. People were important to him: they *mattered* to Jesus.

To be close to people is what the incarnation was all about. 'The Word became flesh and made his dwelling among us. We have seen his glory, the glory of the one and only Son, who came from the Father, full of grace and truth' (John 1:14). In Jesus, God became a man so that he could be close to people. Without question the incarnation of Jesus is a unique event of human history and is of utmost theological, soteriological significance. At the same time, the incarnation is a template, a pattern for church planters to follow in their daily lives. They will want to 'live among' people in their communities. They will want to get close to people, so that those far from God can find their way back to God through the 'bridge' of a relationship.

Theologians of past generations spoke of the 'condescension of God' to describe that God is unapproachable, totally 'other'. Yet he draws near to humankind through the man Jesus. 'Condescension also means that he adopts the living conditions of his human children.'[3]

---

2 Paul M. Zulehner, "Mystik und Politik: In Gott eintauchen, bei den Menschen auftauchen", a speech held in Benediktbeuern, Germany on 19 November 2007.
3 Herbst, p 11.

Planting churches like Jesus did is people-centred work. People are more important than seminars, books, plans and systems. That's why church planting doesn't happen on the drawing board or the computer screen. It happens in real life, in personal relationships with real people. Church planters will do what Jesus did: they will spend time with people. That is incarnational contact.

Principle 2: Motivating Compassion

When we look at Jesus' life and ministry, we notice that he was constantly on-the-go, moving among many towns and villages. Galilee, the northern region of Israel, is where we find him most often. The Jewish historian Josephus, who also held military command over Galilee, approximates that the population was about three million.[4] If we look a little deeper to determine what motivated Jesus, we find it was compassion. People were lacking direction; they were in danger; they were afraid. Jesus compared them to sheep without a shepherd, and it broke his heart (Matthew 9:35–38).

Compassion was the driving force behind Jesus' behaviour. It was what motivated his miracles, and indeed his entire ministry. It moved Jesus to see a widow who, in addition to the loss of her husband, had to bear the loss of her son as well. 'When the Lord saw her, he had compassion for her and said to her, "Do not weep"' (Luke 7:13, NRSV, Anglicized). Jesus had compassion for whole crowds of people (Matthew 9:36) and for individuals (Matthew 20:34). The compassion he felt for an entire city moved him quite literally to tears (Luke 19:41–44). Likewise, his heart felt love for a single affluent young man (Mark 10:21). He taught his disciples to be merciful, as the Father is merciful (Luke 6:36). Moreover, Jesus taught them that compassion is an inherent element in God's judgment: those who clothe the naked, visit the imprisoned, give food and drink to the hungry and thirsty – those people who are merciful will find favour with God (Matthew 25:34–36).

---

4 In *Vita*, par 45, Josephus writes of 240 towns and villages in Galilee. In *Bellum* III, iii, 2, he writes that the smallest of these villages had more than 15,000 residents. We can thus calculate that according to Josephus the region of Galilee had a population of more than 3,000,000 people.

Johannes Reimer writes about the importance of compassion in the life of a church:

> *The church is the people of God for a needy world. That's why nothing does her more credit than compassion. Twice Jesus quoted the passage from Hosea 6:6: 'I desire mercy and not sacrifice', in Matthew 9:13 and 12:7. Mercy focuses its attention on the sick and the sinful (9:12 ff.) and does not condemn the innocent (12:7). Mercy seeks out those in need and tries to meet the need (Matthew 25:31 ff.). Compassion shapes the internal life of the church by lifting up the last and the least and not overburdening them; and compassion determines the attitude of the church toward outsiders as well (Matthew 25:31 ff.)[5]*

Many ministries in our established churches as well as in church planting are being done with an amazing professionalism. Never before in church history has there been such an emphasis on excellence and quality in ministry as there is in our day. This is not a bad thing, unless it's accompanied by a loss of compassion. Professionalism devolves into idolatry if those involved in ministry no longer have their hearts broken by the knowledge that people are far from God.

Principle 3: Christ-Centred Proclamation

Why did Jesus spend so much time with people? Why was he so concerned for them and for their lack of direction? Being close to people and feeling compassion for their situation loosened Jesus' tongue. More than 100 times we read in the Gospels the three-word phrase: 'And he spoke'. And what Jesus said was nothing short of sensational. 'They were astounded at his teaching,' was people's reaction to Jesus' words (Mark 1:22, 27, NRSV, Anglicized). Jesus gave his followers the assignment to proclaim the gospel to all nations and to every creature (Mark 13:10; 16:15), because he himself proclaimed the good news. Indeed, he *was* the good news.

---

5 Reimer, p 64.

The healings, casting out of demons and many signs and wonders that Jesus did were astonishing, but without some explanation as to their purpose, they would have been nothing more than sensational. Coupled with the news that Jesus was the Son of Man, the Messiah, the hope of the world, his miracles had a far greater purpose. Jesus made it clear that he intended to proclaim the good news of the arrival of the kingdom of God in this world: 'I must proclaim the good news of the kingdom of God to the other towns also, because that is why I was sent' (Luke 4:43). Jesus understood that he was the subject of his own proclamation.

He was the King of the kingdom whose coming he announced. The Church Father Origen described Jesus as the *autobasileia*, i.e., the 'self-kingdom', the kingdom in his own person. He preached the message of the kingdom of God in synagogues (Luke 4:44), in the temple (Luke 20:1), in all the towns and villages in Galilee (Matthew 9:35), on the shores of the Sea of Galilee (Luke 5:1), and on a mountainside (Matthew 5:1). Ultimately he commanded his disciples to proclaim the message of the kingdom throughout the whole world (Matthew 24:14).

The content of Jesus' teaching and preaching was the kingdom of God. 'Jesus went into Galilee, proclaiming the good news of God. "The time has come," he said. "The kingdom of God has come near. Repent and believe in the good news!"' (Mark 1:14–15). 'But if it is by the Spirit of God that I drive out demons, then the kingdom of God has come upon you' (Matthew 12:28). Jesus preached the kingdom of God so that people would receive the kingdom, so that they would allow the kingdom to shape and direct them. In God's kingdom, Jesus is the King – he wants to be king in our lives, and in our world as well.

When we pray, 'Your kingdom come', we are not asking for God's kingdom to become a reality. It already *is* a reality. We're committing ourselves to live in God's kingdom reality in *our* lives, in *our* world. We're committing our lives and our world to be gripped by God's kingdom. We're committing ourselves to be changed by the Kingdom. We're committing the trajectory of our lives and the trajectory of our world to be re-directed by the kingdom of God.

There's a widespread misunderstanding among Christians in this regard. Some think like this: 'God took the initiative and came to us in our world. Jesus gave his life on the cross in order to bear our sins and remove our guilt. To become a Christian, we have to receive Christ and his work for us. Jesus is active. We are passive. Jesus offers us forgiveness and a place in heaven, and we gladly accept.' Many Christians 'let God in', and may try to be friendly and nice, but they remain in charge of their own lives. They make their own plans, and then they ask Jesus to bless their plans.

What Jesus taught about the kingdom of God and life in the kingdom is, however, quite different. The kingdom of God *comes* to us in Jesus. Suddenly the King is here. He's active in us, and his activity has its effect: his activity activates us. This, after all, is the source of the freedom we experience – the freedom to live differently by the power of God. Jesus is not visible as he was when he lived with his Apostles on the earth. But he's with us, just as surely as he was with them. He teaches us how we can live his life in this world. When we become Christians, we become Jesus' apprentices – a disciple is a learner, a student, an apprentice.

The point of Jesus' teaching was always Jesus himself, because he was and is the point of salvation. Unlike the prophets in the Old Testament, he did not talk about one who was yet to come to save people. Instead, he said that *he himself* was the promised Saviour.

Principle 4: Liberating Lordship

The reason people flocked to Jesus was that he was so different. His person, his teaching, his claims were all different from anything they had ever experienced before. Jesus lived and taught in ways that were contrary to what his contemporaries believed was right. We see this distinction sharply in Jesus' choice of his disciples.

There were many religious teachers around in Jesus' day, and they all had their own groups of apprentices or disciples. It was a standard practice for aspiring disciples to have to apply to be accepted by a particular rabbi. The best-known and most highly esteemed rabbis accepted only the best students, those with the most promising futures. Many an aspiring young disciple had to pursue another career path because they did not meet the high standards set by the rabbis.

That is why his Jewish contemporaries were astonished, perhaps even scandalized, by Jesus' choice of disciples. Jesus didn't wait for students to apply. He approached individuals and called them to follow him (Mark 1:17; 2:14; 3:13–14). The people he approached and called to follow him were individuals who would never have stood a chance with other rabbis. Jesus chose people who were not particularly significant in the eyes of society: fishermen, tax collectors, resistance fighters, hotheads, uneducated misfits. What mattered to Jesus was not an impressive looking résumé but the simple willingness to *follow* him.

The good news hasn't been fully proclaimed unless Jesus' claim to lordship in the lives of his followers is included. 'Why do you call me "Lord, Lord," and do not do what I say?' (Luke 6:46). Jesus has a right to expect a life lived under his influence and lordship because he claims to be God. When he said, 'before Abraham was born, I am' (John 8:58), he was claiming to be equal with God. 'Anyone who has seen me has seen the Father' (John 14:9). Thomas, the once doubting and later believing disciple, fell to his knees before the resurrected Jesus and said, 'My Lord and my God!' (John 20:28). To claim to believe the good news without accepting Jesus' right to the authority of Lord and King is twisted indeed.

When I'm in conversation with people about the gospel and matters of faith, I often hear them say, 'But I believe in God.' They want me to know that everything is fine between them and God. They're in good standing with him. I congratulate them for believing in God and then take them to the passage in James that states, 'You believe that there is one God. Good! Even the demons believe that – and shudder!' (James 2:19). It's no great shakes to believe in God. Even the devil believes in God. Actually, the devil could probably teach a pretty good theology class. The difference between a devil and a Christian is not so much between their belief systems as between their lifestyles. Devils resist Jesus. Christians submit to Jesus and his lordship, and this shows itself in their behaviour. Faith in Christ always affects life and behaviour. The conduct of Christians bears witness to the fact that Jesus is Lord and holds sway in their lives. 'Why do you call me "Lord, Lord," and do not do what I say?' (Luke 6:46).

The lordship of Jesus Christ in the life of a Christian is simply the logical consequence of discipleship. Jesus calls us to follow him and thereby become his disciples. And it is exactly this follower-ship, this discipleship, that frees people from their old way of life and sets them on the way to follow God. As Hesselgrave puts it, 'Converts' and 'believers' *as popularly conceived* might 'do their own thing'. But 'disciples obviously must do the will of their Master'.[6]

Principle 5: Changed Identity

The man born blind and healed by Jesus reached a two-fold conclusion. For one thing, he recognized who Jesus was, and for another, he recognized who he had become because of Jesus (John 9). His understanding of who had healed him developed gradually: first he referred to him as 'The man they call Jesus' (John 9:11). Later he told the Pharisees that Jesus 'is a prophet' (John 9:17). Later still he told them that Jesus was 'from God' (John 9:33). And then the unthinkable happened: 'they threw him out' (John 9:34). Because his parents had feared this would happen to them, they refused to give the Pharisees any information, for 'the Jews had already agreed that anyone who confessed Jesus to be the Messiah would be put out of the synagogue' (John 9:22). Today in the 21st century we can hardly imagine how severe the consequences of such an expulsion would have been. Back then, for a Jew to be put out of the synagogue meant to lose his place in society, to be treated as if he were no longer be a Jew but a foreigner. It meant that he lost the acceptance of family and friends. Worse yet, it meant he would be cut off from God. When the Pharisees threw him out of the synagogue, this man lost his identity. In many ways, for him it was the end of the world.

Jesus finds him in this miserable condition and asks him, 'Do you believe in the Son of Man?' To which he responds, 'Who is he, sir ... Tell me so that I may believe in him' (John 9:35–36). Jesus lets him know that he himself is the Son of Man, the Messiah. The man then turns to Jesus and says, 'Lord, I believe,' and worships him (John 9:38). He had lost his identity, yet now he receives a new identity in Christ Jesus.

I think John included this incident in his Gospel account because he wanted to convey an overarching truth. The story of the man born blind, healed by Jesus, expelled from the synagogue, and then given a new identity in Christ is a parable of the life of every Christ-follower. Education,

---

6 Hesselgrave (1980), p 23.

heritage, wealth, achievements and reputation – none of these determine our identity any longer. They've been replaced by Jesus. In Christ Jesus we know who we are, to whom we belong and why we are here. Our outward circumstances may remain the same, but our self-awareness, our self-image, our sense of identity is radically different. We have become Christians because we have been given life by Christ himself.

It was similar when Jesus called the first Apostles: 'He went up the mountain and called to him those whom he wanted, and they came to him. And he appointed twelve, whom he also named apostles, *to be with him*, and to be sent out to proclaim the message, and to have authority to cast out demons' (Mark 3:13–15, NRSV, Anglicized; author's emphasis). Here we see a calling and a commission, and we must never confuse the one with the other. The calling is to be with Jesus. The commission is to preach and to do the works of God. Our first and only calling is to be with Jesus. We dare not make the mistake of trying to carry out the commission without living out the calling.

The first question every person has to answer is the question of identity: 'Who am I?' Those who don't know Jesus often look inside themselves for their identity and find no clear answer to this fundamental question, 'Who am I?' The truth is, the answer to the question of our identity always lies outside ourselves. Everyone who becomes a Christian receives a new identity. By knowing Christ, we come to know ourselves: our identity is in Christ.

There were many occasions when Jesus emphasized this teaching about the changed identity of his followers. He told Nicodemus, an educated Pharisee who was a sincere seeker of the truth, 'No one can see the kingdom of God unless they are born again' (John 3:3). This new birth occurs 'of the Spirit' (3:8). From above, from God himself, who is the creator of spiritual life, arises a new family relationship within the kingdom of God. Eight times in this section we find the term 'born' or 'born again'. Jesus used this language to describe what it's like to enter the kingdom of God.

In another instance, Jesus' mother and brothers were looking for him. Jesus turned to the crowd gathered around him and, looking at *them*, he said, 'Here are my mother and my brothers! Whoever does God's will is my brother and sister and mother' (Mark 3:34–35). Those who do the

will of God have a new identity in Christ. They're his kin. They belong to
his family.

We also find this teaching of a new identity in Christ in the familiar
words of the Great Commission. Jesus commanded us: 'Baptize them in
the name of the Father and of the Son and of the Holy Spirit' (Matthew
28:19). Those who, acting out of their own volition, are baptized, become
the property of and participants in the fellowship of the triune God. All
who are baptized are in fellowship with God. They share in the very life of
God. They are citizens of God's kingdom and members of God's family.
They have an entirely new identity.

Why is it so important for church planters to understand the reality
of a person's new identity in Christ? Because understanding this truth will
shape our understanding of the nature of the church we are starting. And
we only want to plant churches that follow God's plan and are filled with
his power. If people do not grasp the fundamental importance of their
identity in Christ, if their life and ministry is not based in this reality, then
a church is no different from a club or any other organization, it is simply
a collection of people who share a common creed or experience. But the
church as Jesus envisioned her is radically different. The church is a miracle
– the miracle of belonging to the God of the universe, and together with
others being part of God's reality, sharing in the miraculous work God is
doing in this world. The church is a new spiritual community where every
member has been made new and given a new identity.

Principle 6: Practical Discipleship

Viewed from a sociologist's perspective, the first disciples were a prototype
of the church. Jesus chose twelve men who would turn the world upside
down. What kind of people were these men? Thomas was a melancholic
skeptic. Judas was a greedy traitor. Peter was reckless and impulsive. The
brothers James and John were headstrong cholerics. Simon was an idealistic
resistance fighter who hated paying Roman taxes. Matthew was a man who
exploited his own people and loved the Roman system of taxation because
it made him rich. These twelve were an explosive mixture! And yet it was

these men whom Jesus hand-picked to form a community that would be a model of unity and love.

Jesus made them his disciples. He chose them to carry out his work. The assignment Jesus gave to the church is to make disciples. With this in mind, it's fair to paraphrase Matthew 28:19–20 as follows: 'While you are going [into all the world, and in your daily activities], train them [anyone willing to become a disciple] as apprentices, immerse them in the reality of the triune God [in the Hebrew, the term *name* is equivalent to the *person*], teach them to do everything I have told you. And know this: I will *always* be with you.' A disciple of Jesus will make other people into disciples, too. It's really that simple. To accomplish it, however, requires concentrated effort on our part.

Disciples who make new disciples is the goal of church planting. People who have come under the lordship of Christ and have found a new identity in him learn to live as he lived. That is why we do not just want to call people to 'make decisions for' Christ. Rather, our aim is to make people disciples, so that Christ is formed in them (Galatians 4:19).

What did Jesus have in mind when he called people to be his disciples? He wanted transformation (life change), and not a mere transfer of information. The Great Commission instructs Jesus' disciples to 'teach them to *keep* everything that I have commanded you' (Matthew 28:20, author's emphasis). If we are to teach people 'to keep' Jesus' commands, this means we will have to show them how to apply his teaching to the situations of our everyday lives. Bible knowledge alone does not necessarily lead to life change.

For five summers while he was growing up, Elvis Presley attended a Christian camp conducted by his church. He grew up in poverty, and his parents simply couldn't afford to pay for him to go to camp. His church, however, had a solution. Anyone who memorized 350 Bible verses could go to camp for free. Elvis Presley was able to go to camp five years in a row at no cost to his family, because year after year he memorized hundreds of Bible verses. Over a period of five years, he memorized some 1750 Bible verses.[7] However, that knowledge was not enough for him to lead a God-honouring life. Bible knowledge without life change is just a hobby.

---

7 Ogden, pp 43–44.

A disciple is someone who sees the harvest and gets to work: 'The harvest is plentiful, but the workers are few' (Matthew 9:37). Disciples learn how to build relationships with people far from God in order to bring them into close contact with Jesus.

Jesus never thought of discipleship training as a dry theoretical exercise. He took his disciples into real-life situations. His curriculum was simple and effective. He gave his team a brief orientation, sent them to their assigned tasks, and afterwards had follow-up conversations, which were powerful teaching moments. We tend to reverse the order. We give some orientation, then we teach, and then lastly we give the ministry assignments. We often train with the motto: *Just in case* – 'It's possible you might need to know this or that.' In contrast, Jesus trained his disciples with the motto: *Just in time.* What they experienced in the real world of ministry provided just what they needed to learn when they needed to learn it. The way Jesus trained his disciples to be church planters is how we should train people as well: *by on-the-job training* – learning-while-doing.

Principle 7: Empowering Leadership

After making disciples, Jesus made leaders out of them. In the Gospels we see how he often took charge to influence people and to move them to action. At the wedding at Cana, he put his host's servants to work, so that with their help he could turn water into wine (John 2:1–11). The centurion, who had many soldiers under his command, recognized in Jesus his superior officer, because he said:

> *Lord, do not trouble yourself, for I am not worthy to have you come under my roof; therefore I did not presume to come to you. But only speak the word, and let my servant be healed. For I also am a man set under authority, with soldiers under me; and I say to one, "Go," and he goes, and to another, "Come," and he comes, and to my servant, "Do this," and the servant does it (Luke 7:6–8).*

Jesus compared himself to a shepherd who tends sheep that listen to his voice and follow him (John 10:27).

If Jesus had remained alone in his role as leader, if he had not trained his disciples to become leaders, his work would have ended with his ascension to heaven. But because he knew that the church would not survive without gifted leadership, he gave his disciples the authority to lead. He trained them to do what he had been doing in front of their eyes all along – preaching, healing, casting out demons. He gave his twelve Apostles the authority and the power to do these same things, and he sent them out to do them (Luke 9:1–6). A short time later he did the same with a group of seventy-two disciples (Luke 10:1–11). After his resurrection, Jesus gave his followers the authority to make disciples of all the nations (Matthew 28:19–20). He gave Peter, who had failed him miserably, the job of feeding his 'lambs' (John 21:15).

Robert Logan talks about a four-step plan to train leaders, a plan that resembles the pattern Jesus used in turning his disciples into leaders. First, Jesus invited his disciples to observe him doing ministry, and then to talk about it together ('I do something, and you observe'). Next, he gave them a part of the job, while he still did the lion's share of the work himself ('I do something, and you help me'). In the third step, Jesus gave them more responsibility, and he helped them ('You do something, and I help you'). And lastly, he gave them full responsibility ('You do something, and I observe'). After every assignment, the disciples talked with Jesus about what they had done and what they had learned, so that their learning was intensified and multiplied.[8]

Good leaders invest in others so that they, in turn, will be able to do what the leaders had previously done. That is the only way to lay a foundation on which churches can grow and multiply.

Principle 8: Intentional Multiplication

Jesus' beginnings as a church planter were modest, to say the least. He concentrated on the one person who was willing to deny himself, take

---

8 Logan & George, p 95.

up his cross and follow him (Luke 9:2). He started small, but his goal was always enormous. From the very first step, despite modest beginnings, Jesus always wanted to achieve multiplication.

Many of Jesus' parables reveal his keen interest in the expansion of the kingdom of God, and thus also in church planting. Jesus always wanted to see sincere recipients of the good news bear fruit – thirty-fold, sixty-fold, even a hundred-fold (Mark 4:20). Jesus compared his followers to a farmer who plants seeds in a field, seeds that grow into mature stalks of grain and yield a plentiful harvest (Mark 4:26–29). Jesus spoke of the kingdom of God as a small mustard seed that germinates and grows into a tree large enough to provide shelter for many birds (Mark 4:30–32). In all these parables, Jesus makes a connection between small beginnings and bountiful results. Although the initial entrance of the kingdom of God may not seem meaningful, ultimately it will reach global dimensions and lead to the eschatological reign of King Jesus. Jesus' intention has been clear from the beginning: He wants his kingdom to spread to all people of all cultures in every land on earth: 'Go into all the world and preach the gospel to all creation' (Mark 16:15); 'Make disciples of all nations' (Matthew 28:19).

Shortly before he left his disciples, Jesus talked to them about the blessing that they could leave behind: 'This is to my Father's glory, that you bear much fruit, showing yourselves to be my disciples' (John 15:8). He predicted that his disciples would do even *greater* works than he had done (John 14:12). What is the nature of this blessing? Four times in the book of Acts Luke mentions the 'adding' or 'gain' (expansion) to the number of people who became Christians because of the testimony of the first disciples (Acts 2:41, 47; 5:14; 11:24). Then he shifts to a higher gear and talks about growth that is more like multiplication than addition (Acts 6:1, 7; 9:31; 12:34; 16:5). Both the number of disciples and the number of churches grew. That's real growth! These are the works that are greater than what Jesus had done: conversion growth and the daily increase in the number of newly planted churches.

In the seventies, the British theologian J.B. Philipps wrote a book with the striking title *Your God Is Too Small.*[9] It conveys the sense that Christ-followers can be more modest than God intended them to be. Instead of

---

9 See bibliography.

striving to achieve great God-given goals, they are content with minimal results. Robert Logan often said, 'The real fruit of an apple tree is not an apple. It's another apple tree.'[10] Similarly, the fruit of a church is not just measured in more members, but also in more churches.

Summary

Jesus is our ultimate example. In his life and ministry he left us a model for how we can do the work of church planting today. Jesus planted the first church and along the way he trained the first church planters. If we are going to plant new, dynamic and lasting churches in our world today, we will have to learn from Jesus. His close relationship with his Father teaches us that we will never make it in our own strength. His time spent with the Father led him to spend time with people. Instead of in the office, we'll prefer to spend time with people in coffee houses, restaurants and homes. It broke Jesus' heart that so many people were so very lost. What was true for Jesus, should be true for us as well: the eyes that see lead to the heart that is broken (Matthew 9:35–38). For those without hope and direction the message of Jesus was a lifeline: 'People, the kingdom of God has entered *your world*.' It is our job to awaken people's interest in a reality that they have been hitherto unaware of: the reality of the presence and the goodness of God. Jesus led people away from finding their meaning centred in themselves. To seek ultimate meaning in oneself leads to a dead end. We will not just talk about forgiveness from sin and guilt, as important as that is. We will also talk about the need to change allegiance, to allow Jesus to be King and Lord of our lives. The church is the place where we take part in fellowship with the living God. Freed from the props, supports and entanglements of our old life, we find in Christ a new identity as we join the family of God. Jesus taught his disciples to be present in this world in the same way that he was. It is our job to teach people how to live in partnership with Jesus in the reality of their everyday lives. Jesus' eyes lit up when he thought about the potential for his glorious kingdom to expand throughout the whole world as the church grows and

10 Logan, p 24.

new churches are planted. As more and more churches are planted, people on every continent and in every culture are touched and changed by the life of Jesus.

Those who dare to take up the challenge of church planting the way Jesus did it, will experience the highest of highs and perhaps also the lowest of lows in their lives. It will be worth it, though, because Jesus is worthy, and the people he came to redeem are worth risking everything for. Today, just as he did back then, Jesus is looking for that one person who cares about people, who will give God first place in his or her life and, together with others, will move into a broken world to plant the church of Jesus Christ.

In Part II, each element of the Jesus Model will be discussed in greater detail, with many suggestions for practical application.

PART II

THE JESUS WAY:

Practices of Church Planting Based on the Jesus Model

THREE

At Home in the Presence of God the Father

As a church planter, Jesus nourished his soul with his Father's love.

The fundamental food of the church planter is his intimacy with God the Father. That was not always true of me. I had to experience a crisis before I took this basic lesson to heart.

During my internship with the Evangelical Free Church in Frankfurt, the elders asked me to assume leadership of the planting of a new daughter church in the region of the Taunus hills. I was not just excited about this, I was white hot with excitement. After all, this is why I had studied theology for eight years. I dreamed about church planting, talked about it, read about it, wrote about it. It was fantastic to think that I was going to lead a church planting project. I couldn't imagine anything better. We began to meet, pray and plan with a team of twenty-five people from the sending church. In no time at all we sensed that God's grace and favour were with us. We were amazed when the mayor of the city of Oberursel offered us, at no cost, the use of a community centre – the first meeting place for the worship services of our new church! Another nearby church offered us meeting rooms for our children's ministry. Many people agreed to volunteer. Advertising, positive articles in the local press, a spirit of acceptance on the part of other existing churches in the area – everything went unbelievably smoothly. People came, and some of them became believers. Attendance at our services grew, so that within three months we were numbering between 70 and 90 adults.

It was a dream come true. My wife and I prayed, we worked hard, and we were happy. But my joy didn't last long. Within about six or seven months, I began to slip into a mild depression. Internally something seemed to be breaking down. I didn't understand why this was happening to me. I should have been the happiest church planter in the country. But instead, all joy left me. In the middle of this dark time, I made one of the best decisions of my life. I decided to hike through the Taunus hills, alone with Jesus. Taking only my Bible, a notebook and a pen, I started off. I walked for hours along dusty paths through fields and forests. All along the way I kept asking Jesus the same question: *Why?* 'Why am I so sad? I should be happy, but I just feel completely empty, tired, and joyless.'

The Church Fathers of old called this condition *acedia* – a tiredness of the soul. I know that I was also suffering from *anhedony*. The word 'hedonism' describes a life marked by lust and pleasure; *anhedony* is the inability to experience joy. I had accomplished so much already with God's help, and yet I felt as if I had lost something really important.

During the hours of wrestling, God gave me an answer. I read Psalm 42, and suddenly it was as if blinkers fell from my eyes. The Psalm begins with the words of King David, who was forced to flee into the wilderness. He says to God, 'As the deer pants for streams of water, so my soul pants for you, my God. My soul thirsts for God, for the living God. When shall I go and meet with God?' (Psalm 42:1–2) The reason for my *acedia* became clear: I was longing for God's blessing in church planting. I hungered and thirsted for it. But I was not longing for God himself with the same intensity. That was it! I was trying to feed my soul with God's blessing, instead of with God himself. I confessed my idolatry to God – that I had placed doing ministry for God ahead of God himself. Afterwards, something new and beautiful happened inside me. I began to long – sincerely, hungrily, greedily, persistently – for God and *his* presence. My emotional condition changed noticeably. Joy returned.

Via detours like this one, I discovered what Jesus had taught us by his life: the presence of God the Father is the only thing that can sustain happiness and contentment, and only his presence can give us the authority to do ministry and plant churches.

Jesus bathed his soul in the fellowship he had with his Father. The presence of his Father was the source of Jesus' joy and authority. Jesus sought his Father's presence, hungered and thirsted for it. Likewise, healthy church planters will find and guard their joy and fulfilment in Jesus before and during the early stages of church planting, and beyond.

Living with Temptation

Henri Nouwen, in speaking about the temptation of Christ, describes three dangers that threaten to erode the life of our souls.[1] Church planters are particularly vulnerable to these threats.

The temptation to be relevant: turn stones into bread

Christian ministry often leads to low self-esteem. The world looks for competence, and for centuries the church and her spiritual leaders were valued for their particular competence. Unfortunately, this is often no longer the case today. Instead of pastoral counsellors, there are therapists; instead of biblical instruction, there's education; instead of prayer, there's self-initiative; instead of a life based on principles, there's life based on pragmatism. In order to please those around them and be respected, church planters are tempted to primarily rely on skills that society recognizes and rewards, rather than on the power of God.

The temptation to be loved: 'Throw yourself from the pinnacle of the temple'

To throw himself from the top of the temple and be caught by angels – that would have been spectacular! People would have loved Jesus for that. We are in danger of doing things that put us in the limelight. Church planters already stand in the spotlight, they have a public role, they are easily seen by others. Because they are so visible, they experience a strong temptation to manipulate circumstances and people in order to make an even bigger impression.

---

1 Nouwen, pp 27–93.

The temptation to appear powerful: 'Worship me, and I promise you the world'

The temptation to seize power is strongest where human transparency is weakest. Many high-flying Christian leaders are people who are not able to give and receive love. Our personal inadequacies can be masked by working for God.

When Satan tempts Christians today, he directs their attention away from their inner spiritual impulses towards externals. Fire can be extinguished by removing oxygen; similarly, spiritual vibrancy too can be extinguished by focusing too much on externals.

The Bible makes clear that we are to pay attention to the nurture of our souls: 'Guard your heart, for everything you do flows from it' (Proverbs 4:23). 'Pay close attention to yourself and to your teaching; continue in these things' (1 Timothy 4:16, NRSV, Anglicized). The best gift we can give to the churches we are going to plant is that of an ordered soul: the beauty and the power of the gospel should reside in us and be visible in us. The credibility of our message will be evidenced through our relationship with Jesus and with our Father in heaven. But ministry for God done without God will lead to judgment against us.

Longing after God – the Spiritual Disciplines of the Church Planter

Church planters are, as a rule, active people. That is their strength. They are in essence entrepreneurs who risk everything so that good things might happen and people will get connected to God. When they get up in the morning, they are already thinking about what they can accomplish this day. And it is true that they probably can accomplish a lot by their own efforts: ideas flow, people follow them, new projects are started, crises are faced and overcome, many are reached for Jesus. Events are set in motion and people are motivated when church planters get to work.

But, if that's how it works for you, beware, for there will come a day when things suddenly no longer work. This is why it is important for church planters to stay fresh: and they do it through spiritual disciplines. Spiritual disciplines keep them from losing their joy and their authority in ministry, for church planting does not start with a church plant; it starts with a well-nourished soul that is in an untroubled and loving relationship with the heavenly Father.

Everyone who serves people in the name of Jesus will get tired. Ministry includes exhaustion. Jesus often faced many pressures and expectations. He was:

- surrounded by people: 'Everyone is looking for you!' (Mark 1:37)
- tested: 'Jesus … was led by the Spirit into the wilderness, where for forty days he was tempted by the devil.' (Luke 4:1–2)
- abandoned by people: 'From this time many of his disciples turned back and no longer followed him.' (John 6:66)
- attacked by opponents: 'Isn't this the man they are trying to kill?' (John 7:25)
- exhausted from serving people: 'Jesus was in the stern, sleeping on a cushion.' (Mark 4:38)

In times of extreme stress, Jesus often sought fellowship with his Father, on his own, away from other people: it is one of the first spiritual disciplines. A number of different spiritual disciplines (or disciplines for the spiritual life) have been practised not only by Jesus but also by his followers throughout the ages.

A *discipline* is an activity that helps to train us to accomplish something that we could not otherwise accomplish through our natural effort: 'Watch and pray so that you will not fall into temptation. The spirit is willing, but the flesh is weak' (Matthew 26:41). I think 'flesh' here means one's own resources and ability.

The spiritual disciplines can be divided into two categories: disciplines of *abstinence* and disciplines of *activity*.

Disciplines of abstinence

These disciplines are intended to focus and sharpen our spiritual awareness.

Solitude

Definition: To separate oneself voluntarily for a time from people and things in order to have more space for God. In solitude we resist *doing* things in order to get a result. The essence of this discipline is to free ourselves from the pressure to respond to people and things.

Jesus withdrew from the crowds and went into the wilderness (a barren region, Matthew 4:1–2; Mark 1:13; Luke 4:42; 5:16). Moses, too, spent long periods of time on his own (Exodus 3:1). Without the ability to embrace solitude, we will find prayer to be difficult. This discipline safeguards us from prayers that merely hand God a to-do list.

What happens when we stop *doing?* We learn that God cares for us (Leviticus 25:20–22). Solitude reminds me that I have a soul. When I (re-)discover my soul, I discover that God is there: in solitude I am not alone. We will find fellowship with other Christians difficult if we have not learned to live in solitude. Solitude is the foundation for other disciplines – fasting, silence, study.

We must never forget that God does not fight for our attention!

The benefits of solitude are that it:
- breaks the power of hurry and activity in our lives.
- frees us from human dependencies.
- gives us clarity and power to conquer distractions.

Silence

There are two forms of silence: i) to spend time in a quiet place where the only thing we can hear are the sounds of nature; ii) to stop talking.

Silence helps us to relinquish control over ourselves and our environment. It teaches us sober thinking. We come to understand that we are not the movers and shakers of things and people. It helps us remember the power of God, without which we are powerless.

The benefits of silence are that:
- silence frees us from the power of our tongue, which wants to rule our life (James 3:3f).
- self-awareness grows in silence.
- afterwards we will have something to say; then we can speak and bless others with our words (Ephesians 4:29).

Friso Melzer notes the difference in German between 'Rede' (=speech) and 'Gerede' (=idle talk, gossip). 'Gerede' is vacuous, without substance; 'Rede' is substantial, full of content, and it accomplishes things.[2] It's 'Rede' that we need, and this is exactly what comes from solitude: silence teaches us what to say.

Fasting

Fasting means to go without food, in order to experience the full sufficiency of God.

In our Western culture, food is often a tranquilizer – a source of pleasure and personal satisfaction. However the true self is unmasked when we remove food. When we go without the 'medication' of several meals, yet-to-be-dealt-with sins come to the fore – impatience, irritability, anger, self-centredness and many others.

Why is this so? In fasting we acknowledge and experience the reality of another world (Deuteronomy 8:1–6; Matthew 4:4). John 4:32 is an important reference about fasting: 'I have food to eat that you know nothing about.' Fasting can help us find pleasure in Christ, who is the true 'bread of heaven' for us (John 6:31–35). In contrast to the manna, which was perishable, Jesus as 'bread of heaven' offers us imperishable food for our souls. While we are fasting, God becomes our nourishment.

'He humbled you, causing you to hunger' (Deuteronomy 8:3). Humility teaches us to be dependent on God. There are two kinds of fasting: i) disciplinary fasting, in order to learn that God is sufficient; ii) functional fasting (that 'your voice be heard on high' – Isaiah 58:4), in order to bring an important request before God (Daniel 9:3).

Moderation

The renunciation of pleasure as a spiritual discipline frees one from the false security that comes from pleasure. Moderation helps us not to live according to our feelings. In his description of behaviour that will be common in the end times, Paul writes that people will become 'lovers of pleasure rather than lovers of God' (2 Timothy 3:4).

---

2 Melzer, p 215.

Sexual abstinence

To refrain from sexual intercourse and from sexual thoughts as a spiritual discipline trains us not to be controlled by them (Job 31:7–11; Matthew 5:27–28; 19:3–12; 1 Thessalonians 4:1–7). Sexual abstinence teaches us to do without the 'second look'. A temptation may surface when we first notice an urge, a beautiful person, an allure. Inevitably we look. The temptation can lead to a sin if we yield to it. The 'second look' gives expression to the longing for something that is not ours and will do us no good.

Secrecy

In practicing secrecy we prevent other people from noticing our good deeds. In this way we learn to live without the recognition of others. When we do good deeds secretly, we live exclusively in God's sight. We learn to seek approval from God, not from others.

Who am I without recognition? When our hearts are directed toward God, we do not think about what we do in a calculating way (just like the disciples in the story of the judgment of the sheep and goats in Matthew 25: 'Lord, when did we see you hungry ... or thirsty...?').

The best prescription against vanity and pride is to learn to do good deeds together with God but invisible to the eyes of others. Envy and jealousy are both forms of anger. Secrecy chokes envy and jealousy; it frees us from anger.

Sacrifice/Self-denial

In this context sacrifice means giving up what seems (and is) essential to us – money, time, food – in order to learn that God is sufficient (Hebrews 11:17–19). The widow in the story of Elijah gave the prophet her last meal, but then experienced how God supplied her need (1 Kings 17:12–13). Sometimes denial is forced upon us; at other times we do well to choose it voluntarily.

Disciplines of activity

The disciplines of activity include Bible study, celebration, prayer, confession, worship, service, community and meditation. All these disciplines are important, but because they're more familiar than the disciplines of abstinence, and there are many books that discuss how to practise them,[3] I will not discuss them here in more detail.

By making spiritual disciplines part of our lives, we will become more like Jesus.

God-Centred Praying – the Fuel for God's Working

Significant spiritual breakthroughs come when we are dependent on God, which finds its expression in prayer. And it is critical *how* we pray, not just the fact *that* we pray. I am talking about intercession, which, according to Jack Miller, can be divided into two categories: i) protective intercession, where the pray-er asks God to guard or preserve the circumstances (like health, employment, church life); and ii) 'frontline prayers'. Three essential characteristics mark these frontline prayers: the prayer for grace (to confess sins and to humble oneself); the prayer for compassion (and with it for zeal for the whole church to reach out to the lost); and the prayer for a strong desire for God (to see his face and his glory).[4]

Such praying is *vigorous and specific.* It takes God and his promises seriously. Martin Luther was a man who prayed boldly. On June 23, 1540, Luther visited the deathly sick Melanchthon in Weimar. Melanchthon was one of his closest friends and allies in the Reformation. Luther was shocked to find Melanchthon so drastically changed that he hardly recognized him. Luther turned to the window, and then he prayed passionately in a manner that even for him was unusually 'impertinent'. The result of Luther's prayer? Not only did Melanchthon recover from his illness, but he outlived Luther.

Such frontline prayer is *persistent,* and is done by everyone who participates in the work of church planting. Paul challenges us to 'persevere in prayer' (Romans 12:12, NRSV, Anglicized). Why? Because perseverance testifies to our seriousness. Short and quickly forgotten intercession unmasks our independence and self-satisfied attitudes; it denies our devotion to God and trust in him.

---

3 For example Foster; also Willard, *The Spirit of the Disciplines.* Also see Appendix C.
4 Keller & Thompson, pp 207–08.

God-centred praying, as we have seen, *includes repentance and an expression of our longing for God:* we tell God in prayer that we are tired of our own lovelessness, our unwillingness to sacrifice, our lack of joy. Repentance gives expression to our hunger for God. Tim Keller adds that the prayer of repentance and the longing for God are always connected with hope.[5] Because God loves to bring a turn-around when people turn to him in humility and openness, and so their hope grows.

Somewhere deep inside us there is a longing for fellowship with God. We want to come face to face with him. We want to talk with him about our hurts, our needs, our trials and our joys. But often we discover that talking with God does not come easily. We find it hard to pray honestly, openly, single-mindedly. Jesus' disciples had exactly the same problem. They watched him leave early in the morning to go and talk with his Father. When he returned from his time of prayer, they could tell he had renewed power and presence. Gradually they too began to long for such a prayer life. Together they went to Jesus with the request, 'Lord, teach us to pray.' Prayer has to be learned. Whether we are beginners or advanced in the school of prayer, Jesus will teach us to pray. He will show us how and what we should say to God. He taught his disciples the well-known 'Our Father' prayer. It is the pattern that shows us all, including those in the work of church planting, how Jesus prayed for people and circumstances (Matthew 6:5–13). We come before a holy God and call him 'our Father', even 'our Dad'. We are in relationship with the One who has redeemed us. Then we see in the opening sentences that the heart of every Christ-follower should beat for God's glory, God's kingdom (lordship) and God's will. Only after these three requests become priorities in our lives can we pray for personal matters: provision, forgiveness, protection. In the same way that we trust our heavenly Father for our day-to-day needs, we should trust him for our emotional and moral needs as well. God is committed to shape us into his image. This process of sanctification will often be unpleasant and difficult, but attaining a new quality of life will make it all worthwhile.

'I believe it is more difficult to pray the Lord's Prayer than to win all of Napoleon's battles,' wrote the poet Friedrich Hebbel.[6] The seven short

---

5 Keller & Thompson, p 207.
6 Letter to Pastor Luck dated 21 January 1861.

requests of the Lord's Prayer are rich in content. As a result, this prayer model is as suited to the beginner as to the advanced pray-er. A person who is speaking to God consciously for the first time in her life can follow the pattern of this prayer, and the mature Christian who has walked with God for a long time and has a rich history of life experience with God, will yet continue to discover new and fresh challenge and comfort in this prayer.

The church planter in the presence of God the Father

Church planters should learn to become strong pray-ers. Likewise, they should work to build a team that lives in God's presence. Prayer is the fuel by which God shows his activity. Who are the people who are suited for a church planting team? For one thing, they will be people who have a passion for Jesus and who demonstrate this in their praying. We learn a lot about people when we listen to them pray. In addition, it should be people who have certain social skills: a positive attitude towards serving, and a humble spirit. Humble people are teachable. Good team members see what needs to be done and lend a hand without being asked. They are able to recognize the critical issues and to give their honest opinion, as well as make a contribution towards solving the problems. These people have a positive attitude toward life, combined with a trust in God's power and faithfulness.

And what about the leader of a church planting project? What characteristics are needed for him or her? The leader will have a visible love for God as Father, as well as a strong love for people. This person will be a gifted communicator and will have analytical skills, too. People must want to follow him or her. A church planter will often have dominant personality traits without being domineering, or a highly integrating and initiating personality.

The well-known DISC profiling tool[7] is helpful in evaluating prospective church planters. The letters in DISC represent the initials of the four basic personality traits which, according to the DISC model, determines interpersonal behaviour: *D*ominance, *I*nfluence, *S*teadiness, *C*onscientiousness. 'By observing concrete situations, the personality

---

7 See Sandy Kulkin, *The DISC Personality System: Enhance Communication and Relationships* (The Institute of Motivational Learning, 2011). Also described in February 2013 at: http://changingminds.org/explanations/preferences/disc.htm

profile delivers to the individual a customized description of his/her own strengths, weaknesses and potentially ideal positions.'[8] People with high scores in Dominance (D) and Influence (I) are more suited to lead a church-planting project than those who score high on Steadiness (S) and Conscientious (C). However, church planters will need other personality types around them to complement or correct them.

Churches that are culturally relevant and life changing are oases in which God's presence is palpable. The nearness of God to the people derives from the nearness of the church planter to God the Father. Jesus established this close relationship as being at the very core of his calling, because it was from this alone that he received the authority and the joy that drew people to him and transformed them. And if that was critically important for Jesus, it must be critically important for every church planter who follows Jesus' calling.

---

8 *DISG Persönlichkeitsprofil,* p 9.

FOUR

Incarnational Approach

Dr Herbert Schnädelbach is a Professor Emeritus of Philosophy at the Humboldt University in Berlin. Schnädelbach is a self-professed atheist. At the turn of the 21st century, he wrote an article in the German newspaper, *Die Zeit,* entitled 'The Curse of Christianity', in which he criticized 'seven birth defects of a world religion that has become old'.[1] Despite his reservations, he is open to the Christian faith. When a journalist asked him what he as a philosopher thinks about the idea that God became a man in Jesus Christ, Schnädelbach replied: 'I confess that the concept of the incarnation of God is the most profound thing that Christianity has produced. That God has become man makes Christianity in the truest sense of the word human. This idea is a revolution in the history of religion.'[2]

The Revolution of the Incarnation

The incarnation is God's revolution for the people of this world. If an atheist recognizes this, how much more should those who are planting churches! Unfortunately this is not always so.

When God in Jesus appeared in our world, he stormed into the lives of mortals with revolutionary change. 'The Word became flesh and made his dwelling among us. We have seen his glory, the glory of the one and only Son, who came from the Father, full of grace and truth' (John 1:14).

---

1 Herbert Schnädelbach, "Der Fluch des Christentums", *Die Zeit,* 20 (2000).
2 Quoted from a personal communication by Karsten Huhn, March 2009.

That's a revolution! In Jesus, God put himself at our eye level. In Jesus, God allowed us to share in his life. In Jesus, God made himself vulnerable, exposed, open to attack. Conclusion: The revolution of the incarnation is a revolution of the love of God. This news is almost too good to be true.

In his last public address at the age of 86, the much honoured and widely respected English theologian John Stott directed a final word to Christians around the world.[3] To encourage and exhort his audience, he chose the incarnation as the central point of his address. First he spoke of the incarnation of God in Christ Jesus as something unique, unrepeatable, unequaled in world history and salvation history. From this starting point, Stott insisted that the ongoing incarnation of Jesus every day in the life of individual Christ-followers is indispensibly important in order to reach the lost. Jesus must find expression every day, in many ways, in his followers if those outside the faith are to develop a deep longing for Christ. And he concluded that God's way to make us like Jesus is by filling us with the Holy Spirit ... a trinitarian conclusion! The billboard for the grace of God is, in the final analysis, the presence of God in the lives, words and deeds of his children. God wants to use people to touch, invite and win over other people. God can unleash a revolution of love in this world when everyday people express his extraordinariness in the ordinary circumstances of life.

As an example of this, I think of a young woman I met who lived for a year in Delhi in India under adverse and dangerous conditions. Why would a young Western woman expose herself to physical and psychological danger in a hot, dusty foreign city? Because of love. The clinic where she worked housed primarily women and children infected with the HIV virus. She loved these women and children. Dying patients experienced the love of God through her caring touch. In order to reach Indian people with the love of God, she became 'Indian': she lived with a Sikh family, dressed like a Sikh woman, ate with her right hand, learned Hindi, spent her time listening, serving and playing with those whom others avoided. Her quiet and kind ways started a small revolution of love, because she lived incarnationally.

---

3 Sourced in February 2013 at: http://www.langhampartnership.org/2007/07/20/john-stotts-final-public-address/

Church planters will seek to live incarnationally among the people to whom they are called.

Evangelistic and Missional Efforts

Jesus was both evangelistic and missional in his approach to his contemporaries. Church planting efforts that are saturated with the presence of God will relate naturally and intentionally to people in ways that are both evangelistic and missional. Evangelistic and missional – what is different between these two terms, and what is similar? Both indicate an orientation towards the lost. Evangelistically- and missionally-inclined Christ-followers pray for courage and boldness to approach non-Christians. They want to be with those who are far from God because they like them. They spend little time in their office and considerably more time in restaurants, cafés and at dinner tables. Both evangelistically- and missionally-inclined Christ-followers want to bring Jesus to people who do not know him, and both want to do it not through events, but through relationships.

However, there are differences between those who are evangelistically focussed in their lives and those who are missionally focussed. Christ-followers who are evangelistically focussed live among non-Christians, want to win them for Jesus, and then integrate them into the church. The local church is their focal point, because for them the church is the place where people grow in their walk with Jesus, discover their gifts, and serve others. In contrast, the missionally focussed look for the *third places* of non-Christians: the places where *they* spend their free time and cultivate their social lives. Missional Christians settle into these *third places,* make themselves at home there, become regulars. Together with other missional Christ-followers, they see to it that new life and the kingdom of God take root there in the presence of non-Christians. New cells of the life of Jesus grow in the *third places* of non-Christians and begin to thrive in places that have been the focal point of *their* lives. These people are not going to enter the world of a Christian church, which for them is foreign territory. Instead, they experience serious discipleship in their familiar surroundings. Evangelistic Christians lead the fruit back into the church. Missional Christians allow the fruit to become fruitful in its familiar environment.

Neither of these approaches should be used on its own. Each needs the complementary aspects of the other. Jesus was both evangelistic and missional as he moved among the people of his time. Sometimes he called people to join him, as the new focal point of their lives. They were to follow him, go where he went, sleep and eat where he slept and ate. The twelve Apostles are examples of Jesus' evangelistic approach. At the same time, Jesus was also missional. He sought out the *third places* of those who were marginalized. He spent a lot of time with them where they were, saw the kingdom of God arise among them, and he left them in their own environment. He wanted his new life to spread among people who had neither the courage nor the desire to leave their own environment to enter a different, already existing community.

Becoming a Greek to the Greeks

An incarnational approach begins with the church-planting team getting to know the culture of their environment. Heinrich Christian Rust puts it this way: 'God's mission happens there where it intersects with the needs of people. However, it's not just the felt needs that are determinative. We have to talk about election and about lostness and about being far from God, even if a person far from God does not recognize that he is lost. We cannot choose between needs-oriented and a commission-oriented mission for the church.'[4] Just like a screw buries itself in the wood, church planters drill deep into the culture. They get to know the people and their circumstances by doing research, but also by spending time with them as interested learners. So they start at their desks in order to end up at the dinner table. In every major city in Europe there is a chamber of commerce, an office of statistics or some similar civic agency. Church planters can find a plethora of demographic information about the city there: demographic trends within the city, and even in sections of the city, are often captured over a period of ten or twenty years; for example, information about the growth or decline of the population, a breakdown of the population in terms of gender, religious affiliation, marital status, ethnicity, the percentages of pre-school children or retirees, single-family homes and apartments, income levels, and even indications of where new

---

4 Rust, p 21.

construction is planned. Demographic information like this reveals where a city is growing and where it is shrinking. Further sources that provide helpful information about the composition of the population include local magazines and newspapers, libraries and the internet.

Psychography provides additional insights beyond the demographics. Psychography examines people's values, feelings and longings. Helpful information of this kind can be found in media packs for local publications, newspapers, magazines, books, scientific studies at universities and from official government statics.[5] Some large commercial chains also have their own departments of psychography from which data can be obtained, usually for a fee.

Conducting your own surveys among the people you seek to reach allows you to rub shoulders with your target audience and gather important information first-hand. When we were still in the preparation stage for a new church plant in Kaiserslautern, we surveyed 500 city residents between the ages of 20 and 45. We had them indicate their education level and their age, in brackets of 5 years, and we asked the following questions:

1. In your opinion, what are the needs of the people in this city?
2. Many people no longer attend church. In your opinion, why is this the case? (We asked this question in the third person, but received answers in the first person. Most people gave us their own reasons for no longer attending church.)
3. What should a church be like, if you were to attend?
4. What time do you usually get up on Sundays?
5. What topics would you like to have addressed in a sermon?
6. What are your hopes for your future?
7. Who are your personal heroes?
8. Are you interested in receiving the results of this survey? (Almost 200 people wanted to receive the results.)

---

5 For example, sourced in February 2013: http://data.gov.uk/about-us See also: http://www.mrs.org.uk/ijmr and http://www.questia.com/library/communication/advertising-and-public-relations/psychographics

Building a network of contacts

Even better than interviews are deep personal conversations with people far from God. Tim Keller recommends having a natural sequence of questions in your head, questions that begin with a person's social context (occupation, education, housing), then progress into the inner world (hopes, fears), touch on the religious life (church, religion), leading to questions of worldview (which aspects of biblical truth or the gospel do they understand, which does she reject?).[6] With questions like these you can learn a vast amount about the people you want to reach.

The results of research like this should not only lead to new insights but also answer evangelistic and missional questions. Based on research results the question arises as to how you can gain access to the hearts and minds of the people you want to reach with the gospel. Where does the team need to adjust in order to become a 'Greek to the Greeks'? What matters to people? What hopes and fears do they have? What barriers to Jesus have they erected around themselves? What gives us credibility with these people? How would Jesus live and speak in their presence?

Research among the target audience leads to a core area of three overlapping elements (see Figure 2). When the gospel intersects with the needs of people in the community and with the gifts and talents of the church-planting team, the foundation can be laid for the birth of a culturally-relevant church.

Jesus' approach to people was personal. He mixed with the guests at a wedding for an entire week. Tax collectors and other despised people found in Jesus a willing conversation partner. And time and again he asked questions that awakened interest: 'Do you want to get well?' (John 5:6). 'Where shall we buy bread for these (5000) people to eat?' (John 6:5). 'Do you also want to leave?' (John 6:67). 'Do you love me?' (John 21:6). 'Why are you thinking these things in your hearts?' (Luke 5:22). We learn from Jesus how we can connect to people.

Whoever sits down with people whom they want to reach for Christ has to become a learner. That is the benefit of being a newcomer. A newcomer can ask questions without anyone taking offense. In my experience, most

---

6 Keller & Thompson, pp 80–81.

people are willing to be helpful when they find someone who is genuinely interested or who is seeking to learn.

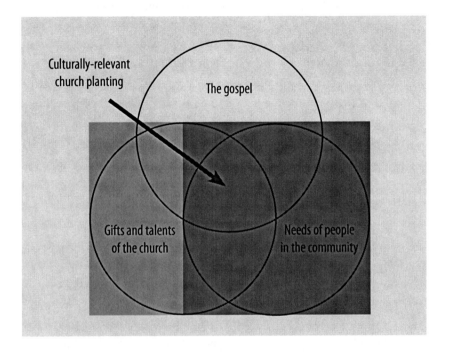

Figure 2: Culturally-relevant church planting[7]

Tim Keller began in just this way when he started Redeemer Presbyterian Church in Manhattan in 1989. He met with people who lived and worked there, non-religious people, and learned from them: what philosophy of life they espoused and why, what cultural events they liked to attend, with what hopes and fears they lived. One conversation led to the next. One person led to the next. Within a few months Keller had built a network of relationships with several hundred people. He learned a lot from them, and they learned to trust him. Because Keller was able to submerge himself in their thought-world and in their geographic turf, he began to understand the life pulse of these downtown New Yorkers and what made them tick.

---

7 Adapted from Reimer, p 236.

Building relationships before starting worship services

One of the greatest mistakes often made in church-planting work is to start worship services too soon. The church planter is new in the area. She hardly knows anyone. Those she does know, she doesn't know well, because she hasn't yet built deeper relationships with them. But she starts offering worship services anyway, and then is surprised that these are not well attended. Often this is attributed to 'hard soil'. The soil may indeed be hard, but that is no excuse for avoiding the difficult yet very rewarding work of building networks of relationships.

When is the appropriate time to start worship services? In my experience, this is not the case until the leaders have each built a network of 50 relationships to those outside the faith. Relationships are the glue of a healthy church. If, in the early stages, leaders are not able to build trusting relationships, it will not happen later either, regardless of how attractive and thrilling the worship services may be. Jesus called us to people, not to events. Frequently, events can become the excuse for not having time to spend with people. Jesus gave himself for people, and we are called to follow him in his devotion to people.

A further reason why networks of relationships with not-yet-believers should be developed can be found in the dynamic of a church. The longer a church is in existence, the stronger the inward pull is on the leaders. The people who already belong to the church have expectations and express desires to be cared for. This is not a bad thing, but it can pose a danger. For if the leadership team has not managed to build and cultivate networks of relationships before the church services start, the growing demands of those already in the church can become so strong that relationships to outsiders never get built.

Let's imagine that entire church-planting teams begin right from the start to live incarnationally among those they want to reach for Jesus. They form missional groups, who through their love and their deeds demonstrate to the lost that they have value. If the team is large, they can divide up into smaller missional cells of five to seven people each.

What to do when you are in the right place

The question is, what do these missional groups do when they're spending time with non-Christians? In a climate of normal human interaction, where interest and excitement for something are predominant – sports, music, fleamarket treasures, art, children – members of the team are on the lookout for signs of the activity of God's kingdom in the lives of their new friends and acquaintances. If we believe that God is always at work through his Spirit, then we can assume that he is also at work in the lives of non-Christians. But they don't know it. When Christ-followers recognize the activity of God, they make their friends aware of it, which is a blessing and an encouragement.

Not long ago I had flown from Frankfurt to the USA and was in Miami awaiting my connecting flight to Orlando. It was after midnight, and the plane was already two hours late. Along with all the other passengers, I was tired. Exhausted. We all just wanted to get this short flight over with and fall into bed. When everyone had finally boarded, we were all seated, except one rather tall gentleman, who was standing in the aisle by the first row, just behind the bulkhead, where the most leg room exists. He was carrying on a heated conversation with the flight attendant, telling her that he had been promised a seat in this first row. But the row was already full. An entire aeroplane with 200 passengers was being held up by this one gentleman, because the pilot cannot start until all passengers have taken their seats. The tension was palpable. Everyone was observing this depressing scene and waiting for a resolution. Suddenly a man in the first row got up, walked down the aisle without a word and took one of the few remaining open seats in the back of the plane. The problem was solved. I admired the courage of this man.

I saw this guy again in the baggage claim area. I went up to him and said, 'Excuse me, but I couldn't help noticing what you did earlier before we took off. I thought it was fantastic and courageous of you to give up your seat to make room for the other gentleman. That was a generous, magnanimous thing to do. I think Jesus would have done what you did. Thank you.' The response on his face showed a mixture of surprise and joy.

When Christ-followers point out the activitiy of Jesus in the life of non-Christians, it spawns an awareness of a new dimension in their life. We don't always have to mention Jesus or God. Sometimes it's enough just to speak about a character trait of God.

Together the missional cell finds a *third place* where people hang out whom they like and want to reach. In places where people far from God like to hang out, there are now also other people, who are Christians. In most Christian circles it works the other way. Non-Christians have to adjust to the environment of Christians if they want to connect with them, because the *third places* of Christians are often worship services and other Christian events. Missional thinkers reverse this procedure, however, and intentionally enter the world of those they want to reach.

Michael Frost believes that eating and drinking belong to a missional lifestyle. In his church in Australia, every church member is encouraged to eat or drink with three non-Christians each week.[8] Life slows down around a meal. Often sociological differences between us disappear: a college student sits next to a senior citizen; across the table a CEO sits next to an employee. It may seem strange, but if only we can discover the power of simple acts like eating and drinking together, we might more often experience God's power to awaken trust in the hearts of those outside the church.

People of peace

While Christians are spending time with non-Christians, they are prayerfully paying attention to certain things. When Jesus sent out his disciples to build networks through preaching and miracles, he gave them a specific instruction: 'Find a man of peace' (Luke 10:6, the author's paraphrase). A person of peace is someone within the target audience whose heart is open towards Christians. A person of peace will be open to trust Christians and can become the gateway to others among his friends and acquaintances.

Malcolm Gladwell describes three kinds of influential people who shape the thinking and behaviour of those around them.[9] His deliniation of these three types of people can help us more readily identify a person of peace. He uses the terms 'connectors, mavens, and salesmen'. *Connectors* are people who, because of their many relationships, connect people with others. If you think of a pyramid, *connectors* are at the top of their social contacts. It's not just that *connectors* know a lot of people. Many of these people live in diverse sectors of society. Then there are the *mavens*. This word comes from the Yiddish, and it means an expert or a connoisseur, someone who also shares his knowledge with others. Gladwell describes

---

8 www.smallboatbigsea.org
9 Gladwell, pp 30–88.

the *maven* as someone who is sought after because of his knowledge, experience or relationships. *Mavens* are people whose opinions influence many other people. According to Gladwell, *mavens* are most effective when they work together with *connectors*. Finally, *salesmen* are people who can convince others of something. If *mavens* contain the databank of helpful information and *connectors* provide the relational web to spread a message, then *salesmen* are the people who can convince others about the message. *Salesmen* convince and create credibility. Because they are persuasive and credible, people follow them.

Gladwell illustrates the power of a *connector* by relating a true story. A young woman in Los Angeles went out to eat with her father, who was a connector. They ate in a Japanese restaurant where the chef was a friend of hers. Her father thought the food was outstanding. On that same evening, he recommended this restaurant to some of his friends who lived nearby. The next day people were queuing up to get into this restaurant. The cause was one man with a gigantic network of acquaintances.[10]

Connectors, *mavens* and *salesmen* can be found in every part of society, in every city or region. They may become people of peace for church planters. If we can win their trust, they will speak well of us and of our plans. Behind every person stands an army of people to whom we suddenly gain access because the person of peace thinks well of us and of what we are doing.

Another example from Kaiserslautern: In the first two weeks after we had moved to Kaiserslautern, I visited the mayor, the vice-mayor, the offices of the local press, and the head of the Protestant Synod. In every case I introduced myself as 'Dietrich Schindler, pastor of the Evangelical Free Church of Kaiserslautern, a church that does not exist yet, but that will exist soon. And this church will be important for the people of this city.' The mayor introduced me right away to the chief of the fire department, who happened to walk by. A journalist asked me about my understanding of my role as pastor. In that year, the local soccer team, 1.FC Kaiserslautern, had won the German national soccer championship under the leadership of their coach, Otto Rehhagel. I told the reporter, 'I'm like a coach who teaches others to live out their Christianity – something like a Christian version of Rehhagel.' Three days later, there was a large half-page article

---

10 Gladwell, p 55.

in the Rheinpfalz newspaper with the headline: 'A Christian version of Rehhagel: Dietrich Schindler wants to start a church – no meeting rooms yet'.[11] That article created a lot of interest and visibility for us among many people. Some of them became our first volunteers.

God's fingerprints

At the same time that missionally-minded Christ-followers are looking for people of peace, they are also looking for God's fingerprints in the lives of non-Christians. Even though there is sin in their lives, people still demonstrate some of the virtues of their Creator. This is a fact of which they are often unaware, so Christians can help them recognize where beauty and goodness are evident in their lives: 'One thing I particularly like about you…'; or 'I've admired this trait of yours. I try to orient my life according to Jesus, but often I see my shortcomings. The way you are helps me to better understand how Jesus wants me to live. Thank you.' These kinds of conversations allow us to be bearers of the hope of the gospel to people who can learn to see their own lives in the light of the reality of God.

Recently a woman poured out her frustration to me. Even though she had often invited her neighbour to special events at her church, and the neighbour responded with a friendly 'thank you', she had never yet shown up at church. With a sigh of resignation, the woman said she wouldn't give up and would be faithful in her efforts. But what if she tried a different tack? She would continue to pray for her neighbour, but in addition she would also begin to pray for herself, asking Christ to give her a sensitivity to recognize his activity in the life of her neighbour. God's fingerprints can be seen everywhere in his creation, including in his (human) creatures, if only we develop an eye for them.

Bad times, great odds

Missionally-minded Christians are also on the lookout for turbulence in the personal lives of their friends. Most people do not want to know about other people's problems. They are put off, repelled by that. But missional Christians tend to be drawn to the problems of others, because when

---

11 *Die Rheinpfalz,* 17 September 1998.

people tell us about their problems, that is a sign of transparency and trust – and a chance to see God at work.

In his farewell address to his disciples in which Jesus spoke about the future of his work on the earth, Jesus instructed them: 'baptizing them in the name of the Father and of the Son and of the Holy Spirit' (Matthew 28:16–20). In baptism, people who have professed Christ as their Lord and Saviour are symbolically baptized into the reality of the Triune God. But before a person can be baptized, he must already have been immersed in the reality of God. Jesus said that this immersion into the reality of God happens while the person is still living without God. The Great Commission says, 'Make disciples of all nations.' Who are the nations? They're the heathen, non-Christians. Discipleship begins before conversion, while people are still living without God.

To hear about turbulence in their personal lives from people who do not believe in God can turn into a wonderful experience. I remember an encounter with Toni.[12] One day I asked him rather casually, 'How are you, Toni?' He responded coolly, 'Good.' Then I dug deeper and said, 'Tell me more.' And then it came tumbling out. He was a locomotive conductor with the German rail system, but he was currently on sick leave because his train had been in an accident, and he was at fault. Toni told me about an upcoming doctor's visit, and he was worried because it was up to the doctor to decide whether Toni would be forced into early retirement. 'Turbulence in his personal life,' I thought to myself. 'Toni, may I pray for you?' 'Sure,' he replied. Then I placed my right hand on my friend's shoulder, lifted my other hand toward heaven, closed my eyes, and began to pray out loud for Toni and his situation. I asked the Lord for peace, direction, provision for the family, God's blessing, and more. I will never forget what happened next. This tall guy, dressed in leather and boots, head shaved, who could drink anybody under the table, and who lived his life far from God, buried his head in my shoulder, embraced me with both arms, hung on tight, and started to cry like a baby. What had happened? In this one prayer, Toni found himself dropped into the presence of the living God, and this encounter with God deeply touched his wounded soul. As far as I know, Toni is still not a Christian, but he now has the feeling that there really is a God.

---

12 Not his real name.

Promptings from the Holy Spirit

In whatever situation they find themselves, missional Christians are constantly listening for promptings from the Holy Spirit. When church planters live their lives devoted to Christ, he will lead them and empower them so that the kingdom of God enters this world. The Bible uses the language of God's *kairos,* his time schedule for carrying out his work with and through the human race. Now it is important that we recognize that God's *kairos* often gets cancelled out by our human *chronos. Chronos* is another Greek word for measuring time. *Chronos* means our appointment calendars, our plans, our schedules. Christians learn to live more by God's *kairos* than by their own *chronos. Kairos* will cost us something, as we see in the story of the good Samaritan. God's *kairos* rarely comes at a convenient time. It tends to upset our usual routines. Neither the priest nor the Levite in the story had the time or inclination to get involved. It was the Samaritan whose behaviour was guided by *kairos.* When we listen to God's Spirit, we will allow our daily schedule to be interrupted in order to serve others in the name of God.

God gave us himself in the person of Jesus. That's the revolution of the incarnation that fascinated Professor Schnädelbach, and it draws our attention as well. That's why the work of church planting begins with building personal relationships. God himself chose this method, and he sends us to the people of our world. In the words of Jesus, 'As the Father has sent me, I am sending you' (John 20:21).

The Four Phases of a Church-Planting Project

Because evangelistic and missional efforts should be coupled with a clear plan for the planting of a church, it is advisable to divide the church-planting process into four separately defined and achievable phases.[13]

Phase 1: Build a start-up team

In order to reach lost people, forming a start-up team is important. Those who are to be part of this team will be completely devoted to Christ, one

---

13 See Fig 3 on p 67, used with permission of Evangelical Covenant Church, USA.
Appendix A contains checklists that the church planter and church-planting coach can use to evaluate progress in each phase.

another and the lost, meaning a start-up team that can be expanded from month to month, rather than a core team that is static and closed. It is the start-up team's goal to develop a unified profile for the new church that articulates the nature, the goals and the methods of the new church: it's essential community, prayer, evangelistic and missional lifestyle. This start-up team should meet twice monthly in an effort to reach consensus on the content of the profile, and to encourage one another to live accordingly. Once a month, the start-up team should invite people from their relational networks to participate in an assimilation activity. These activities can be anything that people enjoy doing together – cooking or extended shared meals, playing games, taking walks, going to concerts or sporting events and so on. The idea is to build relationships with non-Christians and with Christians who are looking for a church.

In the beginning phase of the start-up team, it's important not to allow everyone who wants to join to do so. Strangely enough, church planting projects seem to attract people who have poor relational skills or who have psychological problems. Sometimes Christians want to volunteer, but they have a history of broken relationships in other churches. They have not proven themselves to be capable of working harmoniously with others or of resolving conflict in a constructive way. They see a new church-planting project as an opportunity to jump in and assume responsibility. The discerning team leader will therefore sometimes find it necessary to turn away some willing volunteers, or, in a kind but determined manner, to encourage them to return to their former church. This start-up phase normally lasts six to eight months. The start-up team should have about 15–25 committed members (in rural areas the team could well be smaller). The start-up team should achieve clarity and unity on their vision, values, schedule and strategy. They will begin to discuss the preview phase and consider a financial plan for the church. They will clarify the relationship with the sending church (if there is one), and establish contact with other existing churches in the area.

Phase 2: Start preview worship services

Movie-goers are familiar with trailers that are shown before the actual film starts. Trailers are short clips from forthcoming attractions. They give a preview of what's to come.

Preview worship services have a similar purpose. A preview worship service is one that the start-up team organizes once a month for the people in their relational networks. It is a sample of what the worship services of this church, once it's begun, will be like. Because it happens only once a month, preparing the services will not overload the start-up team. If there is a sending church, it can supply additional volunteers 'on loan' to help in four key areas: music, tech (sound and lighting), children's ministry and food. This kind of support can free the members of the start-up team to give *their* attention to the guests who have come, to build relationships with them.

This phase normally lasts six to eight months. The goal is that 40 to 60 adults attend these worship services. Rural areas will often experience slower growth, and the numbers may be smaller; my figures are based on experience in urban areas. During Phase 2, the regular meetings of the start-up team will continue as before, including the assimilation activities and the work of building relational networks.

Phase 3: Intensification

In Phase 3, preview worship services will be offered twice a month. This helps the start-up team to get used to a regular rhythm of worship services. It is important in this phase to integrate new people; this will happen primarily through relationships. The more relationships those who are visiting the church have to Christians in the church, the more likely it is that they will come back. Small groups and serving groups will also be established during this phase.

It is advisable to plan a start-up celebration during this phase to celebrate the first members of the church declaring their commitment to the church's future. There should be an appropriate programme that has a celebratory feel to it, where the values and goals of the church are emphasized. And of course, great music and good food will help make it fun and festive. Phase 3 also normally lasts between six and eight months, and attendance should grow to between 70 and 100 adults.

Phase 1	Phase 2	Phase 3	Phase 4
Build a start-up team	**Start preview worship services**	**Intensification**	**The grand opening**
1. Identify the church planter and identify an external church-planting coach.	1 \ / 2 \ / 1 3 3 monthly 1 – two preview worship services to show what the church will be like 2 – an assimilation activity (e.g., cookout) 3 – two start-up team meetings for evaluation, preparation and team building	• Increase frequency of worship services to two or three times a month. • Improve quality in every ministry area. • Grow through assimilating non-Christians and unchurched Christians.	Use multiple means to attract visitors: • Use word of mouth, direct mail, printed advertisements, press releases, radio spots, special speakers, etc. • Attract non-Christians looking for answers to the deeper questions of life. • Supplement worship services with special events to increase the church's visibility and maintain momentum.
2. Build a dedicated start-up team that shares the vision, values and passion. 3. Grow through attracting other Christians with similar vision.			

All four stages of church planting as described above, is achieved through:
- Contacts and conversations
- Tell the story as often as possible, why this new church is important (vision casting)
- Practise hospitality
- Hold open-house meetings, inviting non-Christians to mingle with Christians in a home setting – a party, coffee and cake…
- Twice-monthly meetings of the start-up team
- Community-building activities within the team to strengthen relationships

Important note:
i) Emphasize personal invitation (verbal). Other methods can supplement but cannot replace the personal touch of friends inviting their friends.
ii) Strengthen the core ministries: Sunday services, children's ministries, small groups, follow-up with visitors.

Time-frames and projected growth			
5–6 months	6–12 months	6–9 months	4 weeks
Ideally the team doubles in size (to about 20 adults).	Ideally the core doubles in size (to about 40–60 adults).	Ideally the group grows to 40–70 adults.	New church planted…

Figure 3: The four phases of a church-planting project[14]

---

14 Erhard Michel, Evangelical Covenant Church, used by permission.

Phase 4: The grand opening

The final phase is the grand opening. Furniture stores, for example, have shown us how this can be done. When a new furniture store opens its doors for business for the first time, the celebration lasts longer than just a day. Often the grand opening runs for several weeks. The grand opening of a new church should give everyone in the surrounding area a chance to hear about the church, and to know that weekly worship services and other events and services are available. It's important to plan and advertise the grand opening well and to combine it with a number of special events, for there will never be a second chance to make a good first impression.

The start-up team now dissolves and its members become part of serving groups and small groups. Membership is offered to those who attend the church. When a church is planted in this way – with the emphasis on evangelistic and missional lifestyles, combined with a deliberate step-by-step development of structure – it is based on a strong foundation. Sadly, many church plants in the past have lacked such a foundation and have suffered accordingly.

It is important to note that church planting involves more than worship services. We are planting churches, not worship services. Worship services do not make a church. Relationships – Christians to non-Christians, and Christians among one another – make a church. The worship service is one of the most important differences between the ministries of Jesus and Paul. Jesus made disciples without a worship service as the fixed point of their spiritual development, whereas for Paul the worship service played an essential role. Although it's true that the four phases of church planting lead to weekly worship services, it is relationships – healthy, loving, self-sacrificial relationships – that are crucial for the healthy future development of the church, not the worship services as such.

The Four Growth Stages in the Life of a Church Planter

With the planting and growth of a new church, it's easy to overlook something important: the main leader must grow with the growth of the church. She must be able to 'shed her skin' and assume new roles that will make further growth possible. According to Carl George there are four developmental stages or roles that the church planter will need to assume during the growth of the church.[15]

Stage 1: The catalyzer

During the start-up phase and during the first two years of the church, the church planter is the catalyzer. He draws people in and motivates them to commit themselves to something new. The catalyzer is a leader who loves to take risks and start something new. Often he is a person with strong visionary gifts who others want to follow.

Stage 2: The organizer

After the church has been planted, a growing church needs a leader who can transform herself into an organizer. An organizer creates structures, trains volunteers and leaders and ensures that people receive the instruction and coaching they need. The leader herself will now be doing less direct ministry.

Stage 3: The operator

The third developmental stage requires a leader who is an operator, someone who delegates ministry so that he has time to spend with those who lead whole areas of ministry. The leader's success is not measured by the number of people attending church, but by the number of volunteers and leaders who have been empowered to lead in their own ministry areas.

Stage 4: The redeveloper

The fourth stage is that of the redeveloper. This role can be compared with the gardener in John 15. He has to prune the branches so that ultimately they will bear more and better fruit. For the church planter, this means that she has to constantly evaluate the state of the church and take action accordingly. She will eliminate everything that is ineffective. She will renovate and restructure so that the church can move forward effectively. The management consultant and educator Peter Drucker observed astutely that every time an organization doubles in size, half the leaders will not

---

15 Carl George, as quoted by Shenk & Stutzman, pp 176–78.

have the gifts and skills necessary to guide the organization to the next level. The same applies to churches and church growth. Leaders who have reached their maximum potential will have to serve in other ministry areas in order to make room for new leaders who can help the church continue to grow.[16]

So, how do people who are far from God come in contact with him? Through Christians who move incarnationally among them, who share their lives with them. God's great plan to reach the world with his love and grace consists of Christ-followers who embody Christ in a way people can see and touch.

---

16 Peter Drucker, at a pastors' conference, 1990.

FIVE.

Motivating Compassion

His voice was cracking and tears filled his eyes as David told me about their search for an apartment in Hamburg. He and his wife had found one, advertised in the newspaper, that was just what they were looking for. They immediately made an appointment with the agent to view it the following Saturday morning. When they arrived, they were astounded to find 90 other people who were there to see the same apartment. What brought tears to David's eyes was not the hopelessness of their application in the face of so many other applicants. No, it was the realization that most of these people, of a similar age to him, were without a personal relationship to Christ. The vast number of people who lived in Hamburg who were part of their target for ministry moved his heart.

People who want to start a church need to look deep into their own hearts and ask themselves what motivates them. Not every one who wants to start a church does so from pure motives. Some people want to start a new church because they are not satisfied with their current church. They find the people in their current church to be inflexible and tradition-bound. This doesn't suit them. They are more forward looking, thus they want to start a new congregation. Lack of innovation, initiative and vitality in a church may be discouraging, but these are not the right reasons to launch a new church plant.

Other Christians may be in conflict with the leadership of their church. They may feel that their voice is not heard and their opinions are not taken seriously. In order to prove that they do indeed have gifts of leadership and are being underestimated, they opt to start a new church. By doing so, they believe that they give proof that they are more capable than the former church leadership judged them to be.

Through reading the New Testament, yet others become convinced that evangelism and the planting of new churches is God's agenda for today. And because they want to be obedient to God and have been convicted by his word, they set out to start a new church. Or, after thorough analysis, they reach the conclusion that it is strategically important to plant new churches.

Motivations such as these may sometimes be valid, but they are not driven by a deep compassion for the lost. When we look at Jesus, we see that it deeply hurt him to see people around him lost, scattered and living without any clear direction. He ached for them. Certainly we may find church planting to be strategically important or feel compelled to do it as a step of obedience. We may be right to conclude that the leadership of existing churches has no vision for church planting. But these (good) motivations miss the essential characteristic that motivated our Lord: he was moved by deep compassion for the lost. Because compassion was the motive behind Jesus' behaviour, it must be the primary motive for church planters as well.

A Look Beneath the Surface

The following scene is intended to symbolize this concept. It's a quarter past six on a summer morning at the harbour in Calvi on the island of Corsica. With few exceptions, everyone seems to still be asleep. I'm sitting in a comfortable rattan chair enjoying a cappuccino and a croissant. While it is still quiet, I open my heart to God. His words wash like waves over my soul. It's a pleasant and memorable time of reflection.

The harbour in Calvi is really two harbours. In one are anchored exquisitely beautiful sailboats from around the world. The other, directly adjacent to the sailboat harbour, is the dry dock. Sailboats are mounted on large wooden blocks so that their keels can be examined, repaired, sanded and repainted.

To look 'beneath the surface' like this is extremely important for sailing. It is there, where the eyes can not normally see, that cracks occur, mussels attach themselves, and the wood can deteriorate and break apart. A boat can look fantastic up top and yet sink without warning because of failure beneath the surface.

In the same way, our hearts need to occasionally undergo examination in the 'dry dock', where we take a critical look at what lies below the surface of our life. Below the surface, where no one sees, the most crucial things are found: our motives, what drives us, everything that enables us to live our lives.

'Pain, go away!' is something we often say after an injury. It is natural to want to be free of pain. The ability to feel the inner pain of people who are far from God is important, but what exactly do I mean by that?

What is Compassion?

Henri Nouwen was a Dutch-born Catholic priest who embodied the compassion of Christ that church planters need to have in ever-increasing measure. Nouwen was a successful, respected author and a professor at both Harvard and Yale Universities in the USA. His books are bestsellers among both Catholic and Protestant Christians. In 1986, Nouwen, to the surprise of many, left his life as a famous and widely respected professor and submerged himself in a completely new world. From that point on, he lived among mentally handicapped men and women in a community in Toronto called L'Arche. The residents, many of whom could neither read nor write, were not aware of the new pastor's fame. They did not even know what it means to be famous or influential. Nouwen was simply one of them. They patted him on the shoulder, yelled at him, laughed at him, allowed him to help them when they couldn't help themselves. And they loved him.

Through his life among the mentally handicapped, Nouwen learned about compassion. He was amazed at Christ's 'downward movement' and wrote:

> *We see here what compassion means. It is not a stooping down*
> *of the privileged to the level of those without privilege below.*
> *Neither is it a reaching down a hand from those above to the*

unhappy ones far below. Nor a friendly gesture of pity toward those who haven't made it. Quite the opposite. Compassion goes and lives among people and in places where suffering lives. God's compassion is total, absolute, unlimited and unbounded. It is the compassion of those who go to the forgotten corners of the earth and stay there until they are sure that not a single eye is still crying. It is the compassion of a God who doesn't simply act like a servant, but whose behaviour of service is the direct expression of his divinity.[1]

If compassion and mercy are part of the character of Jesus, they should equally be rooted in the character of a church planter. So how can we grow in our ability to be compassionate and merciful?

Right in the beginning of the New Testament, Jesus clearly taught his disciples: 'Be merciful, just as your Father is merciful' (Luke 6:36). When we look at the beginning of the Bible, we immediately read how the first human couple turned against God their Creator. They placed themselves above his rules, tried to hide from his presence and thereby hurt him deeply. A break was caused in the relationship between people and their Creator. Martin Luther later called this *incurvatus in se ipsum* (literally in Latin, 'curled in upon himself'). People without God are on their own, but also curled into themselves and therefore cut off from the life and meaning that comes from a relationship with God. This condition is the result of our human choices and behaviour. We have caused it; we alone are responsible for the heavy burden we bear.

Our human reaction to what Adam and Eve did to their Creator is to condemn them: they are guilty and got what they deserved. However, God surprises us with the paradox of his compassion. When he looks for Adam and Eve in the garden and asks, 'Adam, where are you?', he expresses empathy with the creatures he had made and loves who are in big trouble. *Empathy* literally means 'in-feeling' or 'into-feeling'. An empathic person is able to understand the feelings of others to such an extent that she feels those feelings – she suffers what they are suffering.

---

1 McNeill, Nouwen & Morrison, p 27.

It happened many years ago, but I will never forget this. We were a young married couple with two small children. We had moved into a rental home in a suburb of Frankfurt. After the move there were boxes stacked around waiting to be unpacked. My wife went upstairs to do something, while our three-year-old son Erich remained in the living room. I came in from a quick trip to the hardware store, and I knew immediately that something was not right. As soon as I came through the door, I smelled something burning. While my wife had been upstairs, Erich had found the steam iron, plugged it into the socket and was happily imprinting a new 'iron' pattern into the relatively new carpet. As soon as I walked into the living room, Erich knew that he had done wrong. I turned to him and asked in a calm voice, 'Erich, which would you prefer from me, justice or mercy?' He didn't understand the words, of course, and so he asked, 'Papa, what is justice?' I said, 'Erich, justice means that you will get a spanking, and that you will have to pay money from your piggy bank.' He thought for a minute and then asked, 'What is mercy?' I replied, 'Mercy means that you won't get a spanking, and I will pay for the new carpet.' He thought seriously for a moment before he said, 'I want mercy, Papa.' And mercy is what he received.

God responded to the misdeeds of Adam and Eve with mercy. He did not want to give them what they deserved. It's true that they were punished (they would live at a distance from God as a consequence of their guilt). That is just. But God did not stop with justice. He travelled the path of mercy through Jesus. Jesus announced his primary mission as: 'The Son of Man came to seek and to save the lost' (Luke 19:10). When we approach others who are far from God with such empathy and mercy, we embody the compassion of our Lord.

Interestingly, tolerance or indifference sounds the deathknell for every trace of compassion. The English detective writer Dorothy L. Sayers (1893–1957) wrote not only best-selling novels but also profoundly thoughtful Christian essays. Sayers was particularly damning about the sin of tolerance, or laziness (the sixth deadly sin, called *acedia* or sloth in Catholic theology). Sayers calls it 'the accomplice' of all the other sins and describes it's attitude as caring for nothing, not interested in knowledge, uninvolved, joyless and neither loving nor hating, finding everything pointless and, most distressing, creating in a person a state of mind that 'lives for nothing and only remains alive because there is nothing it would die for'. She points out that our not grasping what mortal threat sloth poses for us, makes this sin the more dangerous.[2]

Tolerance and laziness are opposites of compassion. Compassion empathizes and gets involved. That is what God does, and it is what his children should do as well.

An Example of Compassion: Ruth

Jesus got his compassion for people from his Father in heaven. Humanly speaking, this characteristic was in his genes. Matthew's record of Jesus' family tree names three women, which was not the norm in such genealogies. One of these women was Ruth, who, as a widowed foreigner and refugee, returned with her mother-in-law Naomi to her late husband's hometown, Bethlehem. Ruth, in her compassion (Ruth 1:10–22), is a type of Christ and a model for us.

What happened was as follows: three women – two young and one older – are pulling everything they own in a cart. Life has pummeled them. They have begun a long journey on foot. From the fields of Moab to Bethlehem in Judah – a journey of 70 kilometres. Not far from the border they stop for a rest.

All of a sudden the older woman gets up and cries out, 'This is senseless! Go back to your families! Stay in your homeland! There's no future for you with me. I'm used up. My life is over. But you have your whole lives in front of you. Be sensible! Go back! Why should your lives end with mine?'

Her short speech is incisive and persuasive. It makes sense to one of the younger women, who replies, 'You're right. It really is senseless for me to go with you into the unknown. You make a good case. I'm turning back. Take care!'

One of the younger women leaves, but the other one remains silent. Ruth has decided not to turn back. Come what may, she is not going to leave her battered, bitter, hopeless mother-in-law.

---

2 Dorothy Sayers, from an address given to the Public Morality Council at Caxton Hall, Westminster, 3 October 1941 and subsequently included as an essay, "The Other Six Deadly Sins", in *Creed or Chaos* (1949; re-issued in 1999 by Sophia Institute Press).

How foolish! What kind of young person couples their life to that of a person with no future? In our lives we encounter people whose lives have been trashed. They have gone through one defeat after another. The difficulties they have experienced have made them into difficult people. We may chat with them about this and that, but on the inside, we shut down. We really don't want to have anything more to do with them. They are too much trouble. But compassion knows no such barriers.

Compassion doesn't pay

Of the two younger women, Orpah is the smart one. We would consider her a strong woman. She knows what she wants and what's good for her. After all, who signs up voluntarily for a life of limits and restrictions? Even her mother-in-law Naomi appeals to common sense. Three times she pleads with her daughters-in-law to turn back, because she knows that the compassion they want to show her may not pay off.

Compassion is insane

Naomi's arguments are compelling. She is too old to re-marry. And even if she does re-marry, she is certainly too old to have any more children. She has no more sons, and she will not have any more in the future who could be potential husbands for her daughters-in-law.

To put it plainly: if these women accompany Naomi, they will have neither husbands nor children. In their culture, that was fatal. A woman without a husband and children would have no one to care for her. She would have had no rights and no protection. She would be on the very bottom rung of society. Economically, financially, practically speaking, these women had no future with Naomi. It would not pay to stay with her.

Not only in terms of economics but also emotionally, it would not be easy to stay with Naomi (Ruth 1:20). Naomi was returning bankrupt to her old hometown – financially and emotionally spent. She went to the town hall and applied for a name change. She wanted to change her name so that everyone would know how she was doing. Naomi means 'pleasant', but she felt very unpleasant and instead wanted to be called Mara, meaning 'bitter' (embittered). Life had left a bitter aftertaste in her soul.

It is no fun to live with an embittered person. Such people create a significant barrier to the expression of compassion. But people like Ruth know how to overcome it, instead of being overcome by it.

Compassion appears insane. There are always good reasons why we shouldn't get involved with people in difficult circumstances.

Compassion costs

Compassion is like making a phone call when you have already used up all your minutes. Every additional minute costs you more. There is no such thing as compassion without sacrifice. Ruth considered the costs. Realistically, it wasn't worth it. What would she have to give up? Her homeland, language, culture, hopes for marrige, security and happiness.

Anyone who gets involved in serving others will find himself spent. He will make the payments so that others can receive the dividends. The question, 'What do I get out of this?' is irrelevant. When compassion asks this question, it ceases to be compassion.

Compassion cannot be earned

Compassion does not pay. It is insane. It is costly. And we cannot earn compassion. God's compassion turns our human values upside down: what the world counts as a debit, God sees as a valuable asset.

Ruth's behaviour toward Naomi mirrors God's behaviour toward us. God is by nature compassionate: 'The Lord is slow to anger and abounding in steadfast love' (Numbers 14:18, NRSV, Anglicized).

'Because of the Lord's great love we are not consumed, for his compassions never fail. They are new every morning; great is your faithfulness' (Lamentations 3:22–23). Every morning you receive a fresh load of God's compassion, delivered without charge to your front door!

Compassion is not the result of any formula. It is the unearned gift of God to us. The only requirement is that we find ourselves in a miserable situation, that we be in need and powerless to help ourselves. Many times, it's our own fault; we've painted ourselves into a corner and now there is no way out. And then God shows up. In his compassion, he offers us himself first of all, and then his help. That is grace: God is on our side, through thick and thin. It is fundamentally illogical. Insane. And it is costly: moved by his great compassion, Jesus went to the cross for us.

Compassion sees and acts

Pity and compassion share a deep empathy with those who are suffering. Compassion is distinct from pity, however, in that it gets involved on behalf of the suffering.

It sees the suffering

Compassion begins with awareness. A person and their need are seen. It is a biblical principle that the heart follows the eyes: 'When [Jesus] saw the crowds, he had compassion on them' (Matthew 9:36). What we see will move us.

So how do we go through life? Do we put blinders on and see only those things that appeal to us? Or are our eyes wide open? Do we see people in their pain, and do they matter to us? Ruth saw her mother-in-law's situation and was deeply moved.

It is in solidarity with the suffering

Ruth was able to show compassion because she had made a decision for the living God. Her solidarity with Naomi grew out of her solidarity with the God of Israel. We will never be able to act on behalf of others unless we have made a decision for God. Ruth refused to go with Orpah back to her former life. Orpah turned back to her godless people and their idols, but Ruth chose to not live among a people that had no interest in Yahweh. Ruth did not want to serve Kemosh, the god of the Moabites, a god who demanded child sacrifice.

Ruth made her decision: 'Ruth clung to [Naomi]' (Ruth 1:14). The word 'clung' (Hebrew, *davaq*) literally means to adhere, to stick like glue. Ruth wanted to stick with her mother-in-law. The same Hebrew word is used in Genesis, where it is written: 'Therefore a man leaves his father and his mother and *clings* to his wife, and they become one flesh' (Genesis 2:24). Ruth 1:18 tells us that Ruth 'was determined to go with her'.

If we keep in mind that Naomi was a difficult person, Ruth's unconditional promise to her is amazing. Ruth binds herself to Naomi's destination: 'Where you go I will go.' Ruth binds herself to Naomi's life: 'Where you stay I will stay.' Ruth binds herself to Naomi's people: 'Your people will be my people.' Ruth binds herself to Naomi's God: 'Your God will be my God.' Ruth's commitment has no time limit: 'Where you die I will die – there I will be buried.' And then Ruth solidifies all these promises to Naomi with an oath before God: 'May the Lord do thus and so to me, and more as well, if even death parts me from you' (Ruth 1:17, NRSV, Anglicized). In this last statement we can see that Ruth is already converted, because she uses the personal name of God, *Yahweh*, in order to make clear to whom she must give account.

It engages with the suffering

Compassion is an inner feeling of empathy and a determined choice of the will, but it remains mere pity unless it becomes action. Compassion takes the call, builds up, gets involved, listens, asks questions, and gets to work. Compassion gets moving so that others can progress.

Compassion is in demand

I belong to the generation that grew up with the Beatles. One of their songs in particular found a home in my mind, the song 'Help', from the album with the same name. The lyrics are not complicated poetry, they are not difficult to understand, they express raw desperation: I'm in trouble. I can't fix it myself. I need help. And when a Christ-follower responds to such a cry of help from their neighbour, pain can be eased and the soul refreshed. Compassion is among the most sought-after products to meet the catalogue of human needs today. Everyone longs for compassion, but few can supply it.

Compassion brings renewal

The last verse of the first chapter of Ruth points to hope and renewal: 'So Naomi returned from Moab accompanied by Ruth the Moabitess, her daughter-in-law, arriving in Bethlehem as the barley harvest was beginning.' The author hints that good things are coming for these two women. When God and others show us compassion, we are refreshed. We can breathe again.

We have to ask ourselves, who the Naomis are in our lives. Who is within our reach, who is suffering and needs help? Just as the Lord used Ruth in Naomi's life, he wants to use us in the lives of others. That certainly will not always be easy. It will not always have a happy ending. Sometimes I ask myself: How much disappointment, rejection and setback does God have to deal with because he extends his compassion to us? Why does God allow himself to be constantly rejected by the people he wants to love?

Compassion can be learned
Anyone who wants to can increase their capacity for compassion. How?

1. Observation. Observe how God expresses his love for you. Read the Bible. Additionally, observe others who have the gift of compassion. How do they relate to those in need?
2. Reflection. Think about what you have learned by your observations, and about how you tend to help others. Are there differences? Gaps? What can you work on with Jesus' help?
3. Application. What specific steps can you take, with whom, and when?

Compassion is God-like
Compassion has its origin in God – it is God-like and shows the way God is and the way God behaves.

Compassion identifies biblical nobility
After we've submitted to Christ's leadership in our lives, God begins to change our lives, including the area of compassion. If we return to the story of Ruth, we note that she was able to behave differently because she believed in God. In chapter 3, Boaz praised her for two qualities: 'The Lord bless you, my daughter ... This kindness is greater than that which you showed earlier' (Ruth 3:10). The word *kindness* is translated from the Hebrew word *hesed*. We first see that word in Ruth 1:8, where Naomi says, 'May the Lord show kindness to you.' This blessing worked like a boomerang. It was Naomi who encountered *hesed* when Ruth clung to her. Then, in chapter 2, when Ruth received grain from the field of Boaz, Naomi said, 'The Lord bless [Boaz] ... [The Lord] has not stopped showing his kindness to the living and the dead' (2:20). Finally, Boaz praises Ruth for her love and kindness. The story clearly indicates how those who show *hesed* (Ruth) receive *hesed* (Boaz).

Boaz summarizes Ruth's good qualities and calls her 'a woman of noble character' (3:11). This is an important concept. In the last chapter of Proverbs we find a poem in which each line begins with a consecutive letter of the Hebrew alphabet: the first line begins with *aleph* and speaks of the *eschät hajil* (literally, 'woman of noble character'). Ruth is a woman who personifies the trust in God and the spiritual wisdom that is described in Proverbs.

These are the only two places in the Scriptures where *eschät hajil* is found. It becomes even more interesting to see how the Jews understood this term. There is a different order for the books of the Old Testament in the Jewish Scriptures. The book of Ruth does not follow Judges but instead comes directly after the book of Proverbs. I am convinced that the Jews understood Ruth to be the personification of *eschät hajil*, the woman of noble character. In order to understand Proverbs 31, you have to look at the life of Ruth. She is the model woman of noble character; her faith in God changed her character.

What was so noble about this woman Ruth? It was the way she embodied *hesed*, as if God wanted to say, 'Do you want to know what compassion looks like? Then look at Ruth.' Ruth's attitude points us to Jesus. Jesus was compassionate as his Father in heaven is compassionate.

God's compassion never runs out

When we get involved on behalf of others without having God's involvement in our lives, we will quickly arrive at the end of our inner resources. We will feel empty and burned out. Unless we have experienced the compassion of God ourselves, we will sink when we try to help others. Many of us are hard on ourselves and are surprised when we experience burnout. God shows us compassion. He knows our weaknesses and wants us to be filled and renewed in him before serving others with his love.

A long time ago, an impoverished woman from one of the poorest neighbourhoods of London was invited to spend a holiday at the seaside. This woman had never before seen the ocean. As she stood on the seashore, she broke down in tears. Her hosts could not understand why she was crying. Why the tears, when she was being given a holiday? 'Why are you crying?' they asked. Pointing to the sea, she replied, 'For the first time in my life I see something of which there is enough.'

Our heavenly Father has oceans of compassion. The supply is certainly more than sufficient, and the Father loves to share his compassion with us, and through us to others. His compassion is limitless. What about our compassion? Do people know that we belong to Christ because they can somehow sense Christ in us?

In the context of church planting, compassion can perhaps be compared to hearing the first chords of a well-loved song being played on the radio. We recognize it, even before the lyrics start. Similarly, compassion is the overture to God's grace – when non-Christians hear it, it opens their hearts for the gospel message of grace. That is why compassion is indispensable if we want to plant churches.

SIX

Christ-Centred Proclamation

People We Meet

Decent, helpful, nice people are as a rule not hard to find. They live in terraced houses and apartments in our neighbourhoods. They occupy office chairs in the companies where we work. They are in the classrooms of our universities. They are likeable, and they live according to ideologies or worldviews that our society generally sees as valid. Consider three such worldviews.

1. The hedonist

Hedonism is the pursuit of pleasure as the highest value in life. An addiction to pleasure is now widespread in our society: people are looking for an escape from the bleakness of everyday life. So they immerse themselves in sports, they hop from one party to another, or they seek stimulation through pornography and sex. The pursuit of pleasure becomes a dependency. The body produces adrenaline, which increases a person's sense of happiness.

After every argument with her husband, after every conflict with colleagues at work, Helen gets in her car and drives away. Her destination is always the same: the shopping mall. After she's spent several hundred pounds on clothes, perfume and accessories, she feels better.

Why is it that the pursuit of pleasure always leads to a dead end? Because it makes people prisoners of their moods. When everything is fine, they are quite amiable, but when things are not going well, these people become unbearable. They are captives of their emotions and allow their feelings to control their lives.

This way of life violates the greatest life-giving principle of all: 'Love the Lord your God with all your heart and with all your soul and with all your mind' (Matthew 22:37). Loving God in Jesus Christ gives life and leads to lasting contentment. The pursuit of pleasure makes a person the source of his own life's meaning, and that is a betrayal of God.

2. The materialist

Materialism is the belief that physical objects and possessions are all that matters. The non-material world is perceived to be an illusion, and therefore is unimportant.

The materialist's life centres on their goods. Our consumer society encourages a materialistic philosophy among its members. The hope is that people will buy things not because they need them, but because whatever is new is most exciting. The materialist lives by the motto: 'Whoever has the most toys, wins.'

Why does the pursuit of money or possessions always lead to a dead end? Materialism promises too much and in the end is unmasked as a liar. The thought behind materialism is that things and purchases will make us happy, that therefore they are worthwhile. The truth is that things have no inherent power to make us happy. They have only as much value as people impart to them.

Materialism is blasphemy. The materialist values possessions more than God. Jesus said, 'No one can serve two masters. Either you will hate the one and love the other, or you will be devoted to the one and despise the other. You cannot serve both God and money' (Matthew 6:24). Any object that stands between God and us makes us incapable of unclouded fellowship with God.

3. The altruist

Altruism is the unselfish consideration of others. The altruist lives for the good of others. Surely this is love for your neighbour. So why does altruism also lead to a dead end?

Love for your neighbour, as the Bible describes it, is always a by-product of loving God first and foremost. Anyone who makes love for his neighbour the highest good, when it should be second to love for God, insults God. Love for our neighbour is a by-product, not the centrepiece, of the love for which we were created. That being said, whoever grows in their love for God will automatically grow in love for their neighbour.

What happens when God is our first love, when he has our unconditional devotion and we therefore can love others selflessly? We develop empathy for the people around us. Empathy drove Jesus to compassionate action, to help people and tell them about God and his kingdom.

The Content of the Message

The gospel – what is the good news?

Jesus was inspired by one single idea. Every morning while he was still lying on the hard ground, this was the first thing he thought about. When he was gathering wood for the breakfast fire, and later as he was eating his breakfast fish, this one thought filled his mind. On the dusty streets of Palestine on his way to work, and while washing in the Jordan River, this one thought brought a smile to his face. Every time a child ran up to him, every time he healed someone, every time he cast out a demon, this thought flashed through his head. In every situation of his everyday life, Jesus was filled and animated by the thought of the kingdom of God.

The kingdom of God was the number one topic of Jesus' message. As he began his ministry in Judea, he said, 'Repent, for the kingdom of heaven has come near' (Matthew 4:17). 'Jesus went throughout Galilee … proclaiming the good news of the kingdom, and healing every disease and illness among the people' (Matthew 4:23). Matthew records this account of his ministry in Galilee: 'Jesus went through all the towns and villages … proclaiming the good news of the kingdom and healing every disease and illness' (Matthew 9:35). The Jewish historian Josephus (AD 38–100) wrote that there were 200 cities in Galilee, each with a population of at least 15,000. Even if these figures are from several decades after the crucifixion, it is still safe to assume that within just three years Jesus had travelled throughout a region with a population of three million people. With a sparkle in his eye, he had the same message for one and all: 'The kingdom of God has come.'

In Otterbach near Kaiserslautern, where we used to live as a family, there is a region called 'Himmelreich' (literally, 'kingdom of heaven'). Anyone who has ever been there understands the name. 'Himmelreich' in Otterbach is an area of gently rolling hills, fields and forests. The residents of Otterbach probably chose this name because they thought to themselves, 'Only God could have created countryside this beautiful.'

When Jesus spoke of the kingdom of heaven or the kingdom of God, which is the same reality, he meant something unbelievably beautiful and alive. The reality of this kingdom was so beautiful for him that he told his disciples they should first of all seek the kingdom of God (Matthew 6:33). They were to live intentionally, constantly thinking about the kingdom of God – when they got up in the morning, when they brushed their teeth, drove their cars, did their housework, spoke with colleagues and neighbours.

When we hear the term kingdom of heaven, we immediately tend to think of something foreign to our world. 'The kingdom of heaven – that must be in heaven.' But that is not how it is. The idea of the kingdom of God rocked the world of the people in Jesus' day. And it should rock our world as well.

People were astounded to hear Jesus say, 'If it is by the Spirit of God that I drive out demons, then the kingdom of God has come upon you' (Matthew 12:28). Before a person enters heaven, the kingdom of heaven must first enter her. No one has to wait until she dies to experience the kingdom of heaven. That may sound extraordinary, but it's true! The kingdom of God is present. It is here. It has everything to do with our lives, here and now, and finding it is the best thing that can happen to us.

What's the big deal about the kingdom of God?

Some years ago I was traveling through a remote region of Ethiopia accompanied by my son, Lukas, who was 15 years old at the time. After a long trek on foot over mountainous terrain, we arrived exhausted at the home of some missionaries. Our friend Ruth Weber showed us our accommodation, a small adobe brick house adjacent to a clinic. Even within the walls of this simple house, we were in a world that the local people could hardly imagine. They lived in grass huts with an open fire in the middle of the floor. No chimney. Everybody in one room, as well as smaller animals. If you tried to explain that there are homes where water, even hot water, flows out of pipes in the walls, where heat exists without an open fire, where food can be kept cold in an appliance we call a refrigerator, they would hardly be able to understand it. We noticed that some people who came to the clinic did not know how to open a door. They had never seen a doorknob. They could not even imagine something like a shower or a toilet. But they exist! There are such things as toilets and showers. When Jesus told people about the kingdom of God and said that this kingdom had arrived, here and now, the people thought, ' This is simply too good to be true.' But it *is* true: the kingdom of God is real and among us.

Jesus proclaimed the gospel of the kingdom. Gospel means 'good news'. But what is so good about the kingdom of God? Look at the following four aspects.

i) Living from God's generosity

In Matthew 13:38 Jesus spoke about the 'people of the kingdom' who live in this world. People of the kingdom are teachers, insurance agents, housewives, students, academics, and hospital patients. They see the kingdom of God as a priceless pearl for which it is worth giving up everything to obtain it (Matthew 13:45–46), because they live under the grace of God. God's grace is the unmerited generosity of God that we experience in Jesus.

In the Middle Ages people were afraid of two things: enemies and famine. How good then to live under the authority of a king, because a king gave his subjects the two things they longed for: protection and land. Because of the king, they were protected from their enemies, and they could plant crops and harvest food for their families.

A citizen of the kingdom of God lives every day under the grace of God. Every day, free of charge, Jesus delivers God's forgiveness, peace, strength, joy and other good gifts.

ii) Living under God's influence

'If it is by the Spirit of God that I drive out demons, then the kingdom of God has come upon you' (Matthew 12:28). Why did the evil spirits have to flee? Because they could not stand up against the influence of God in Jesus Christ. They had to capitulate. To come under the influence and power of God is a beautiful thing. Lots of good things happen.

In my experience, as people we are all looking for the same things: for security, peace, fulfillment and acceptance. What many people do not realize is that they can find what they are looking for in Jesus. But in order to discover this, they must first place themselves under the influence of Christ. It is not bondage at all; it is freedom, the ability to finally live the life for which we were created. This is why the Church Fathers spoke about Jesus as the *autobasileia* – Jesus *himself* is the kingdom of God. Everything that God offers us in his grace, everything we long for, is in Jesus.

iii) Living in community with God

In the Lord's Prayer we pray, 'Our Father in heaven … your kingdom come, your will be done, on earth as it is in heaven' (Matthew 6:9–10). In the original text, the word 'heaven' is not singular but plural. Jesus wanted us to know that our Father lives in 'the heavens'. The Jews of the first century believed in three heavens: the first heaven was the atmosphere between earth and the clouds; the second heaven was everything between the clouds and above the clouds; the third heaven was the place where God lived.

In the Lord's Prayer, Jesus wanted us to know that our Father is present in all the heavens, in every part of the atmosphere. In other words, our Father is right now, at this moment, in our atmosphere, as close as the air we breathe. Why? Because he's our Father. Good fathers want to be near their children. Our heavenly Father is a very good father; he wants to be near us.

iv) Living in God's service

Because the disciples were under the influence of Jesus, because they enjoyed the closeness of his presence, because they lived from his generosity, they could do what Jesus did. At the feeding of the five thousand, and later the four thousand, Jesus said to his disciples, 'You give them something to eat.' Jesus did the miracle. Jesus fed the multitudes. But the disciples fed the multitudes as well. By doing this, the disciples were the hands and feet of God: God serves people through other people who live under his influence.

There is a prayer that can help us to live under his influence every day: 'Lord, I seek your kingdom, because I live in your kingdom.' We can pray this simple prayer wherever we go: along the streets and pavements, at work, mornings in bed, silently while we are in conversation with people. 'Lord, I seek your kingdom, because I live in your kingdom.'

Occasionally I have been asked, 'Got Jesus?' The only one clear answer to this question if we are Christians is, 'No.' *I* don't have Jesus. Jesus has *me*. And because he has me, I live in his new reality, which is called the kingdom of heaven or the kingdom of God.

Knowing this, we can live more intentionally. We can start thinking what Jesus thought about all the time: the kingdom of God. We can learn to live from his generosity. We can place ourselves under his influence every day. We can enjoy the nearness of the presence of the heavenly Father. Wherever we go, we are Christ-bearers: *'Lord, I seek your kingdom, because I live in your kingdom.*

Steps to nearness to Christ

It was not enough for Jesus when people understood what the kingdom of God meant. They had to choose the kingdom for themselves, which is why Jesus said that people had to receive the kingdom of God 'like little children' (Matthew 18:1–3). This is the only way a person can enter into God's reality. The way to receive the kingdom of heaven is the path of repentance – turning from a self-directed life to a Christ-directed life: 'Repent, for the kingdom of heaven has come near' (Matthew 3:2). Jesus also described repentance (making a U-turn) as self-denial: a person decides to follow Christ and take up his cross daily (Luke 9:23). Christ-centred proclamation has nothing to do with the communication of particular content; it is the call to choose a life that has Jesus as its new focal point.

In the 1970s two missiologists named Norton and Engel studied the phenomenon of people converting to Christ. Their research and their conclusions are still relevant for the proclamation of the gospel today. The key insight of their research was that people come to faith in Christ through a process of consecutive realizations. The missiologists developed the 'Engel Scale',[1] which depicts the steps that lead to conversion. By using this scale, a numerical value can be placed on a person's proximity to Christ. The

---

1 Engel & Norton, p 45. Also see, for example (live link in February 2013): http://www. xaatuva.com/resources/discipleship/The%20Engel%20Scale.pdf

Engel Scale helps us to ascertain where a person is on her spiritual journey and what can be expected from her.

Value	Spiritual Condition	Possible Alternative Response
+5	Intentionally trains others in discipleship	
+4	Actively shares the gospel with others	
+3	Achieves a certain level of spiritual maturity, discipleship	
+2	Incorporation into a local church, possibly baptism	
+1	Post-Decision evaluation, confirmation of decision, possibly baptism	
Conversion: decision for Jesus		
-1	Challenge and decision	Decides against Jesus
-2	Understands the need for a personal decision	Decides against Jesus
-3	Grasps the implications of the gospel	Decides against Jesus
-4	Understands of the basics of the gospel	
-5	Some awareness of the gospel	No further interest
-6	Aware of the existence of Jesus Christ	
-7	Has no awareness of the existence of Jesus Christ	
-8	Knows nothing of the existence of Jesus, the Gospel, or Christians	

Figure 4: Steps in conversion, based on the Engel Scale

Several years ago, I was talking with an engineer called Tom about the gospel. Tom's wife, Diana, had made a decision for Christ in our church in Mannheim. The change in Diana's life intrigued her husband. Tom began to come to our church with his wife. Over a period of three years, I kept asking Tom the same question: 'Tom, how are you doing in your journey towards Jesus?' I wanted him to understand that he was on a journey, and that the destination was Jesus. And then he would tell me what he thought, where he was still having problems, and why he was not yet ready. I will never forget the phone call that I received from him on a Monday evening. He called me and said, 'Dietrich, I wanted you to be the first to know: I'm going to become a Christian on Thursday evening.' I was really happy that his journey was finally reaching its destination, but I was puzzled why he was not going to take this important step until another four days' time. 'Oh,' he said, 'Thursday evening our small group meets at our house, and

I want to make this decision with my small group here, in front of my friends.' And so the leader of the small group was able to lead Tom to Christ with a simple prayer.

If we are going to plant new churches, proclaim Christ, and invite people to turn to Christ and enter the kingdom of God, then we should understand proclamation.

Forms of Proclamation

Proclamation in its most mature form communicates empathy: it speaks about Jesus Christ. Empathy is the front door of proclamation; it always opens opportunities for proclamation. So it was with Jesus, and it is how now it should be with us as church planters: 'When Jesus landed and saw a large crowd, he had compassion on them ... So he began teaching them many things' (Mark 6:34).

Fresh, relevant, amazing, personal, moving, life-changing – these adjectives describe our Lord's teaching. 'There are three kinds of preachers: those you can't listen to, those you can listen to, and those you must listen to.'[2] People had to listen to Jesus. They were spellbound (Matthew 7:28; 22:33). Jesus' teaching caused amazement and transformation.

When the Bible speaks of proclamation, several different Greek words are used. *Lalein* is the normal word for 'speaking, talking or saying', as in, 'Then Jesus said (*lalein*) to the crowds and to his disciples' (Matthew 23:1).

Dialegomai describes a debate or a discourse that is intended to convince the listeners. Literally *dialegomai* means to 'talk through' something. The disciples argued with one another on the way to Jerusalem. Jesus noticed, and we read, 'On the way they had argued (*dialegomai*) about who was the greatest' (Mark 9:34).

Didaskein is the communication of a written teaching. At the beginning of Jesus' Sermon on the Mount, for example, we read, 'And he began to teach (*didaskein*) them saying...' (Matthew 5:2). The *didaskalos* was the teacher. In this capacity we read, 'Jesus went into the synagogue and began to teach (*didaskein*)' (Mark 1:21).

---

2 Robinson, p 167.

Euangelizo is the proclamation of a positive, heartening message of victory or salvation. When the disciples of John came to Jesus and asked him about his identity in order to alleviate the doubts John the Baptist was experiencing in prison, Jesus told them, 'The blind receive sight, the lame walk, those who have leprosy are cleansed, the deaf hear, the dead are raised, and the good news is proclaimed to the poor (*euangelizo*)' (Matthew 11:5). Our English words 'evangelize' and 'evangelism' come from this Greek term.

Lastly there is the word *kerysso*. 'In those days John the Baptist came, preaching (*kerysso*) in the Desert of Judea and saying, "Repent, for the kingdom of heaven has come near"'(Matthew 3:1–2). Or Jesus' disciples: 'They went out and preached (*kerysso*) that people should repent' (Mark 6:12). *Kerysso* was a public proclamation that was made to the citizens by a herald or public official.

This short discussion of the various Greek words that have been used in Scripture for speech or proclamation can be instructive. The variety of expression indicates that proclamation (of the gospel) is not (only) the responsibility of trained theologians. Most of the instances quoted from the Gospels were not formal preaching situations but common situations in everyday life. People talk with others, face to face. They discuss, argue, persuade and share the good news. In the context of church planting, proclamation has to become rooted once again in everyday language and lived out in everyday life. And yet, there are different ways to communicate Jesus Christ to those around us. In addition, certain styles are more suited to some people than to others.

The Emmaus principle

After his resurrection, while the people of Jerusalem were in an uproar, Jesus joined two men who were walking home to Emmaus. Jesus acted as if he had no idea what was going on. The men told him what had happened in Jerusalem, that the prophet Jesus had been crucified and that some of the women had reported that he had risen from the dead (Luke 24:13–35). As Jesus walked with them, he told them what the Old Testament said about his suffering and his resurrection. When they arrived home, he went inside with them and ate with them until their eyes were opened and they recognized him. From this encounter we draw what I have called 'the Emmaus Principle'. It is relation-intensive and suggests a process of recognition that leads to faith (also described in the Engel Scale).

The principle of cultural relevance

Usually people will not be interested in our message unless we are first interested in *them*. In order to gain access to people's hearts, we have to enter through the door of their felt needs. In other words, we must design our church planting to be culturally relevant. Through conversations with local residents, maybe based on information we got from earlier demographic and psychographic research, we will discover deeply felt needs among the people we want to reach. If we are able to offer people a compassionate touch when they are suffering, we will ease their pain and at the same time gain the credibility that we need if we are to be heard.

A few years ago my colleague Professor Johannes Reimer did some research for a church-planting project in a village with a population of 1800 and discovered a truly unmet need. His team learned that the local soccer team had to get by without showers and a dressing room. After practice or games, the players had to drive home to shower and change. Using their own resources, the four-person church-planting team built a dressing room and showers for the soccer team. A real need was met, and a hearing was won for the message of the church-planting team. Other church-planting teams have found their way into the hearts of people by offering after-school help with homework, financial and marriage counseling, youth work, or by cleaning up playgrounds and other public facilities, as well as many other culturally-relevant activities.

The principle of multiple methods

In the world of fashion, garments are made in different sizes, since of course one size does not fit all. In the proclamation of the good news, a church-planting team will not want to limit itself to one method or style of communication. The more 'ramps' church planters can construct for connecting the lost with the good news, the more people will be reached. The day of distributing printed materials about faith and the church at an information stand at the weekly market, in the hope that people will gladly pick them up and read them, is past, or at the very least it is an insufficient method because it is too one-dimensional. Church-planting teams today must find multiple ways to access the hearts of people with the gospel. Personal evangelism, one-on-one in everyday life, servant evangelism, evangelism through events like concerts, special speakers, worship services, celebrations, and also the use of the internet with live streams and video clips are examples of the many facets of communication we can use to win people today.

The principle of natural style

I was 15 years old when I became a Christian. The very next day, I went door to door with a friend, knocking on the doors of strangers. I wanted to tell them about my experience with Jesus and share with them the 'Four Spiritual Laws'. I was terribly nervous, but I also had a blast! I discovered that I was suited for this kind of evangelism. That was the beginning of a long season in my life when I regularly went to the malls, alone or with other Christians, in order to start conversations about Jesus with people I did not know at all. For certain, many of my readers cannot imagine doing something like this themselves. Why not? Because this style does not fit who they are.

Each of us has a natural style, given to us by God, which can be used in the communication of the gospel. Our job is to identify our own style and to put it into practice consistently. Bill Hybels describes six different styles of evangelism that are found in the Bible.[3] It is useful to find out what style is most clearly suited to you and how you may apply that style in your own evangelistic efforts.

i) Peter's confrontational approach (Acts 2)

The Apostle Peter stood up in public in Jerusalem at Pentecost and boldly proclaimed Jesus as the risen Lord and called his audience to repent and turn to Christ. This style is open, direct, and it does not pull any punches. People who have this style like confronting others. They enjoy going on the offensive when they talk about faith. The amazing thing about people who have this style and employ it, is that they are listened to, and are taken seriously by those with whom they speak.

---

3 Hybels, *Bekehre nicht* [*Becoming a Contagious Christian*], pp 137–52.

ii) Paul's intellectual approach (Acts 17)

The Apostle Paul was well acquainted with the Greek culture and the many gods represented by statues in the area around the Areopagus. He was familiar with the philosophies of the Athenians he wanted to reach. In the 1970s and 1980s, Francis Schaeffer led many intellectuals to Christ at L'Abri, his 'shelter' in Switzerland. People with an intellectual style are apologists. They love to find compelling arguments to convince others of the credibility of the Christian faith.

iii) The blind man's testimonial approach (John 9)

The man who was born blind and who received the gift of sight by Jesus' miraculous healing told others about Jesus based on his own experience with Christ. He told people what his life was like when he was blind, how it came about that Jesus healed him, and who he believed Jesus to be. (There is a notable progression in his understanding, based on how he refers to Jesus: the man – a prophet – come from God – the Lord.) When people simply tell how they themselves became Christians, they speak as experts, for their experience is theirs alone. No other person has come to Christ in exactly the same way as he or she has.

iv) Matthew's interpersonal approach (Luke 5)

Levi the tax collector found Christ and proceeded to invite all his many friends to a lavish party so that he could introduce them to Jesus. The fact is, most people who become Christians do so because a friend has led them to Christ. Each of us has a network of relationships – friends, acquaintances, relatives – and among them are people who do not know Christ. Sometimes God uses our proximity to people like these to draw them to himself.

v) The Samaritan woman's invitational approach (John 4)

The Samaritan woman who spoke with Jesus at the well started believing in him, went back into the town, and told everyone: 'Come, see a man who told me everything I've ever done. Could this be the Messiah?' (John 4:29). Many non-Christians say that they would attend church if someone would invite them. I know several people who are Christians today because they accepted the invitation of a friend to attend a worship service or a small group.

vi) Tabitha's service approach (Acts 9)

Tabitha (also called Dorcas) was known for her 'good works and acts of charity' (Acts 9:36). Her advertisement for Christ was her service to others. Her generous and selfless behaviour caused others to be interested in getting to know Christ. Her quiet, behind-the-scenes, loving service to others was an effective testimonial for the gospel.

How comfortable do you feel sharing your faith with non-Christians? When have you last led someone to Christ? It appears that the majority of church members have delegated the task of evangelism to preachers and other professionals.[4] The majority of Christians have simply withdrawn from all evangelistic activity. Church planters will have to ensure that each person in their team knows their own personal style of evangelism and takes their responsibility for evangelism seriously.

Yet it is also true that the public proclamation of the gospel and Bible teaching by trained Christians has grown in relative importance. Church planters, whose job includes preaching and teaching, have an enormous responsibility to ensure that their teaching and preaching is clear, Spirit-led and Christ-centred.

Considerations for the church planters who teach and preach

The personal preparation of the teacher

Philip Brooks formulated one of the most familiar definitions of Christian preaching: 'Preaching is the communication of a message through a personality.'[5] The message-bearer is the preacher (or teacher). Long before the message-bearer works on the text and the sermon, she must work on herself. If she is comfortable in the presence of God, her life will be open before God and her soul will be clean and ordered. God must first have

---

4 See for example, link live in February 2013:
http://blog.christianitytoday.com/ctliveblog/archives/2012/08/majority-churchgoers-never-evangelize-lifeway-ed-stezter-study.html
5 Brooks, p 8.

gripped her heart, before she can become God's messenger to transform others. We call this an 'authentic' or 'integrated' life before God and others. Teaching always includes both the packaging and the contents: the life of the teacher is the packaging, and the content must include authenticity and credibility.

The goal of proclamation: life change

Jesus ended his famous Sermon on the Mount with a call to action. The difference between the man who built his house on the rock and the one who built on sand was not information. Both builders heard the same message. No, education is not the goal of Jesus' proclamation. Life change is. 'Everyone who hears these words of mine and acts on them will be like a wise man who built his house on rock' (Matthew 7:24, NRSV, Anglicized). Good preachers are always able to answer three questions in their sermons: What? So what? And, what now? 'What?' has to do with the content of a Bible text: what was the biblical author trying to say within the context of his writing and his culture? After people have understood what the Bible text says, we ask the question of relevance for our time and our culture: 'So what?' How important for people to see the beauty, the logic, the genius, and the power of God's word! And the final question, 'What now?' addresses the question of how the text can be applied in real life. Will our listeners know how they can put the teaching of this passage into practice in their daily lives? The result we hope for through this kind of preaching and teaching is life change among the audience.

Proclamation in accordance with ELDA

John Stott often reminded his listeners and readers that a person who wants to proclaim the gospel must first do 'double listening' – to the word of the Holy Scriptures and to the contemporary world (with differing degrees of respect) – in order to apply biblical truth sensitively to the current situation.[6] When God's word penetrates a human heart, it is because a teacher or preacher has succeeded in building a bridge between the world of the Bible and the hearer's everyday life. How can we be sure that this happens?

---

6 Stott, p 10. See also John Stott, *The Contemporary Christian: An Urgent Plea for Double Listening* (UK/USA: IVP, 1992) p 13.

Before we start talking about methods of preaching, note one of my fundamental principles: it is a sin to bore someone with God's word! We may bore people with our holiday snapshots, or with the weather forecast, or with tales of our latest accomplishments – but never, ever must we bore them with God's word! God's word contains refreshment for a society that has become apathetic. Preaching and teaching, done by someone who is on fire for Jesus, can awaken listeners from their lethargy, refresh their hearts and change their lives.

How can we find pointers to enable us, with the help of the Holy Spirit, to do this effectively? I'd like to suggest a simple formula for life-changing proclamation that I call ELDA – *E*xciting, *L*ogical, *D*ecisive, *A*ppealing.

Exciting

In order for an audience to find a sermon exciting, the preacher must first discover the excitement. He or she can find excitement in two places: in the text itself, and in people's lives. When we are studying a passage in the Bible, we will be on the lookout for excitement. What are the high points? Where is the conflict? Where do we find other statements in the Bible that seem to contradict the statements in this passage?

Look at 1 John as an example. In 1 John 1:10 we read, 'If we say that we have not sinned, we make him a liar, and his word is not in us' (NRSV, Anglicized). From this text we can conclude that Christians are sinners. Otherwise Jesus would not have died in their place on the cross. But then we read in 1 John 3:6, 'No one who abides in him sins' (NRSV, Anglicized). From this text we can conclude that Christians do not sin. So we have a problem. And such a problem in the text creates suspense for both the preacher and the audience. Once we have discovered the suspense, we resolve it through an explanation of the verb tenses used. In 1 John 1:10 the verb is in the past tense; in 3:6 the verb is in the present tense. The present tense in this context means that sin no longer belongs to the lifestyle of the Christian. Sin has lost its lasting power, even if the Christian still sins now and again.

Another area where the preacher will find excitement is in people's lives, beginning with his own life. The Bible passage will provide truths through which the preacher can enter people's lives by asking, for example: What questions does the passage raise? Where does it elicit complaints or objections? When preaching about the Lord's Prayer, for example, I often ask the audience: 'Is it a good thing to include Jesus in our plans?' After they have pondered this for a moment, and many people are nodding their assent, I say, 'No, it's not good to include Jesus in our plans!' As already mentioned, Jesus does not want to be included in our plans. He wants to include us in *his* plans.

Logical

When we proclaim the message of the gospel, people should be able to recognize how logical it is to believe that it is true. It has to make sense if people are going to be willing to participate. C.S. Lewis once wrote that he believed in Christ and Christianity in the same way he believed in the sunrise: 'not only because I see it, but because by it I see everything else.'[7] A statement like that can help people understand a passage like the one in John 1:4, 'In him was life, and the life was the light of all people' (NRSV, Anglicized).

Decisive

'So what?' is the question that leads to decisiveness. How did people back then respond to the sayings of Jesus? What historical or present-day examples do we find for someone accepting or rejecting a particular statement of Christ's? What difference would it make in the life of a church or of an individual to live according to Jesus' teachings?

I once preached a sermon entitled 'Patience for the Beginner and the Experienced'. I based the sermon on Galatians 5:22, and I used an example that was intended to awaken a response of decisive action:

Not long ago it was in all the papers: A male nurse, 41 years old, father of three children, won a record 37.6 million Euros in the lottery. Now just imagine for a moment that there were two winners. Both have their winning tickets officially certified. Both go to take possession of their winnings. The first one receives a cheque for 37.6 million Euros. The second one receives an infinite supply of patience. The first one is happy as a king. The second one is bewildered and sad.

---

7 Lewis, *The Weight of Glory*, "Is Theology Poetry", p 140.

The first winner starts buying things that he's always wanted: a big house, a big boat, a new car, a second home on an island, a membership at the country club, and season tickets to the games of all his favourite sports teams.

While he is spending all his money, the second winner begins to exercise patience. Now fast-forward about ten years. The first winner is complaining about his high taxes. He recognizes that many of his friends are only interested in him because of his money. He and his wife had got so entangled in their affluence that they have drifted apart. He feels increasingly lonely and bored. Confused, he looks up to the heavens at night and wonders what his life would have been like if he *hadn't* won the jackpot. And the second winner? He has done and is doing things that he never dreamed possible. He stuck it out at the university, got good grades and a degree, and found a good job. His marriage is getting better all the time ever since he started listening to his wife instead of criticizing her. He discovered an inner longing to help the poor and disadvantaged. He is astonished by the joy and peace in his heart ever since he began spending time with Jesus regularly. His home is often filled with guests who just stop by because they simply enjoy his friendship and that of his family. Bewildered, he looks up to the heavens at night and wonders what his life would have been like if he *hadn't* won patience.

If you should ever have the chance to choose between millions in a lottery jackpot and millions' worth of patience, choose patience, because patience is priceless.

Appealing

A good sermon always concludes with movement. The preacher invites his audience to take the words they have just heard and to internalize them and to put them into practice. The invitation is the challenge. The preacher identifies a vision of a more desirable future in the text, and then asks people to make that *their* future by deciding to live that way *now*. The style of the invitation depends on the statements in the passage. It intends to call forth application in real life – 'What now?' The goal of biblical preaching is always life change.

Although good teaching – teaching that brings to life the importance of God's word and elicits life change – is a gift from heaven, it does not simply fall from heaven into our laps. Intense prayer for illumination and insight, both into the text and into the lives of the hearers, is what unleashes God's blessing.

SEVEN

Liberating Lordship

The church is not an institution but an organism. The church belongs to the Lord. For this reason, from day one the emphasis in a church-planting project is on Jesus Christ as the Lord who sets his followers free. A healthy church-planting culture, where the dependency is upon God and not people, is always underscoring the lordship of Christ, so that churches can be formed by him, filled by him, and sent by him, to do his will.

Sometimes we are able to see profound spiritual truths when we look through the eyes of children. C.S. Lewis, a professor of English literature, was a master of spiritual depth, which he was able to communicate through children's stories, such as *The Chronicles of Narnia*. In these stories we meet a girl named Jill. At one point Jill is enormously thirsty. She finds a stream, but the stream is guarded by a mighty Lion. Jill stands frozen in her tracks. Then an interesting dialogue develops. Jill tries to get a promise from the Lion that it will be safe to approach, but the Lion simply says he cannot make such a promise. She says in that case she will go elsewhere. But the Lion assures her there is no other stream.[1]

Whoever wants the stream must approach the Lion, exactly what people, like Jill, try not to do. They want to enjoy the benefits of the Lion's lordship – the stream – without subjecting themselves to his power.

But the stream and the Lion are inseparable. The stream quenches our thirst, satisfies all our longings, heals our pain, forgives our sin, provides security and gives us lasting peace. We were made for this stream. Our soul cries out for this thirst-quenching stream. But we cannot have the stream

---

1 Lewis, *Der Silberne Sessel* [*The Silver Chair*], pp 21–22.

without the Lion. It is the Lion who gives us access to the stream in the first place. Without the Lion, the benefits of the water would not exist. The Lion awakens in us both hope and fear.

A Disciple's Decisions, Step by Step

Jan David Hettinga was a young Canadian Baptist pastor. He was still relatively inexperienced in ministry when a crisis hit his life. It happened this way: in the tradition of his church, it was normal to invite people to make a decision for Christ at the end of every worship service. So he gave an invitation each week, and was astonished by the response. After almost every sermon, people trusted Christ. Yet his joy didn't last. He realized that many of these people, who had given their lives to Christ, stopped coming to church after a few months. 'What's happening is normal,' a colleague told him. 'It's the same everywhere. If you manage to keep 10 per cent of those who become Christians, you're doing well. You should be happy.' Hettinga was dismayed. The high rate of relapse among those who had newly come to Christ bothered him. He began to read the Gospels with new eyes. He wanted to see how Jesus called people to himself, and what the gospel message really was. What he discovered changed everything: Jesus called people to place their lives under his lordship and leading, and not simply to enjoy his forgiveness or healing.

He noticed that people seemed to become interested in the gospel only when they were sick of their sin. They wanted to be free from their sinful behaviour and its consequences. They took hold of the gospel as God's means to release them from the unpleasant pressure of sin and guilt. At some point after they were sorry for their sins and had been forgiven, their interest in the Bible, church and discipleship diminished. Hettinga saw that Jesus called people to surrender control of their lives. Jesus can only use a person in the ministry of his kingdom when that person has placed herself under Christ's lordship and is willing to be led by him.

Hettinga writes about what he calls a kind of short-circuited understanding of the gospel: 'Although this error in logic is obvious, few notice it. Somehow it doesn't seem strange to us to believe in an all-powerful God, to whom we owe our very existence, and then to live as though we had everything under control. This is in fact the norm.'[2] In a drawing, Hettinga shows the various levels of decisions that a Christ-follower can make. His drawing makes clear that Jesus called people to take up discipleship and not simply to be set free of their burdens.

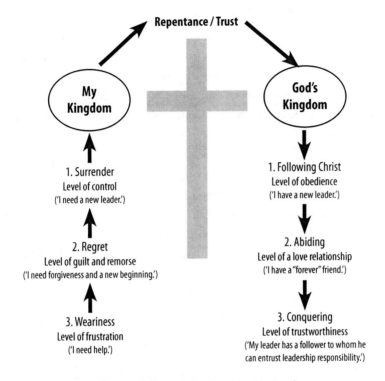

Figure 5: A disciple's decisions (after Hettinga[3])

The telling point about this diagram is the division into two kingdoms. There may be people who have professed Christ as their Saviour and Lord and yet have retained control themselves over how they will live their lives. Jesus called people into a relationship in which the followers exchange their own ways for the ways of Jesus (cf. Luke 9:23–25). Repentance and faith, therefore, mean that a person has let go of his egocentric life and has placed himself under the saving and directing lordship of Jesus.

---

2 Hettinga, p 22.
3 Hettinga, p 105.

Jesus wanted people to live in dependence upon him. Now, as then, this begins with trust. The Jewish concept of trust, which Jesus articulated, was inseparable from the concept of faithfulness. Anyone who entrusted herself to Jesus also remained faithful to Jesus. To trust someone without being faithful to him would have been unthinkable.

We can trust Jesus Christ, because he has proven himself to be trustworthy. Many people who followed Jesus when he was alive on earth did so because of his miracles and other amazing works. He healed lepers, gave blind people sight, stilled storms, drove moneychangers from the temple, turned water into wine, and spoke in a way that enraged some of his listeners. For them, he was the Lion, who succeeded at everything he undertook. His words and deeds of power were impressive. A large part of the crowds who followed him was made up of curiosity seekers and profiteers: 'A large crowd kept following him, because they saw the signs that he was doing for the sick' (John 6:2, NRSV, Anglicized).

Power makes an impression, but it does not automatically lead to trust. What made Jesus trustworthy was his weakness. He often told his disciples about the suffering that awaited him, but they would not believe it. (Would we have been any different, had we been in their place? I doubt it.) After Simon Peter confessed, on behalf of all of them that Jesus was God's Messiah (Luke 9:20), Jesus told them about the suffering that awaited him: 'The Son of Man must suffer many things and be rejected by the elders, the chief priests and the teachers of the law, and he must be killed and on the third day be raised to life' (Luke 9:22). Rejection, derision, death – signs of weakness. Yet it was exactly Jesus' weakness that strengthened the disciples' devotion. After his resurrection, at nearly every encounter with his disciples, we read that they fell down before him and worshipped him (Matthew 28:9, 17). Worship is an expression of trust and faithfulness. Worship happens because Jesus made himself trustworthy by his death *for us* on the cross. Yes, Jesus is the Lion who is powerful, but because he allowed himself to be wounded on our behalf, we can trust him without reservation.

A Change of Lordship

The disciples' behaviour grew out of their relationship with Jesus. Similarly, the Ten Commandments do not start off with the laws but first state the relationship between the people of Israel and Yahweh, their Liberator: 'I am the Lord your God, who brought you out of Egypt, out of the land of slavery' (Exodus 20:2). It was the relationship to Yahweh that determined their behaviour: 'You certainly won't need any other gods besides me, will you?'

In this way Jesus introduced himself to his Jewish contemporaries. He spoke to the Jews who had 'believed in him' (John 8:31): 'If you continue in my word, you are truly my disciples; and you will know the truth, and the truth will make you free' (John 8:31–32, NRSV, Anglicized). The relationship to Jesus frees his followers from the bonds of sin and its dominating power in their lives. Unless a person is connected to Jesus, he will remain a slave of sin. Sin will dictate his behaviour and control his life. However, Jesus called himself a son. A son has rights and privileges that a slave does not have. A son can do something a slave cannot: a son can grant freedom. 'If the Son sets you free, you will be free indeed' (John 8:36). But this freedom from the power of sin can only be enjoyed through a connection to Jesus. It is important, right from the start, for us to speak about the change of dominion necessary for Christ-followers – the necessity of placing ourselves under the lordship of Christ.

When individualists become Christians, they will tend to think of freedom in an individualistic way: 'I'm so happy that Christ has freed me from the burden of my guilt, that he has given me an eternal future with him. I am free – free to walk new paths and discover new ways of self-fulfillment that are good for me and do no harm to others.' People who think like this – and there are plenty of people who come to Christ and do think like this – have yet to understand the freedom Jesus had in mind. The freedom of a Christ-follower is to be liberated from self-determination and to be liberated for life lived to the glory of God the Father. When I become a Christian, I am finally rid of myself – my self as the centrepiece of my existence and the driver of my life. At last I learn what it means to stop insisting on *my* will, and, with God's help, to seek instead *his* will, his glory, and his kingdom in my life.

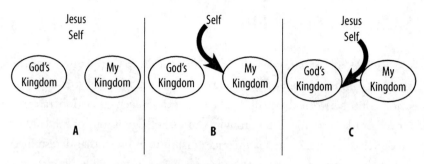

Figure 6: His kingdom come

Let's imagine how a false understanding of freedom can slip into a person's way of thinking or even into the life of a church. The drawing in Figure 6 shows two kingdoms: my kingdom, where things go according to my will; and God's kingdom, where Jesus rules and his will is done (A). Generally, a person starts in her own kingdom and begins to establish it. She dreams of a pleasant life and makes plans to fulfil those dreams. But then this person turns to Christ, and to use a familiar biblical phrase, she 'receives Jesus' (John 1:12). Jesus enters her life. What some people then think, without actually saying it, is: 'Come into my life, Lord Jesus, and help me to build *my* kingdom. Realistically, I know I'm going to encounter situations that are beyond me, where I lack sufficient strength or I simply need the help of Providence. When that happens, I will call on you and ask you to help me' (B).

By now we realize that such an attitude is not Christian at all. In this scenario, self is at the centre, not Christ. This person has allowed herself to be given a Christian varnish, but she is still as self-determined as before. The Bible wants nothing to do with this kind of arrangement. Quite the opposite: Jesus calls us to enter his kingdom and allow him to rule, allow him to give us our purpose, goals, and the strength to do *his* will (C). The test of true discipleship is whether we are ready to do what he asks: 'Why do you call me "Lord, Lord," and do not do what I say?' (Luke 6:46).

How important it is to emphasize the liberating lordship of Christ right from the beginning of a church-planting project and not wait until the church has begun to grow. The team and each additional person need a clear understanding of discipleship. And discipleship will prove itself by the practical outworking of Jesus' lordship in the lives of his followers. Disciples live to please their Master and to be like him in everything.

Church is not the goal of God's mission. Church is rather God's
instrument, with which He seeks to reach His goal. That's why
you can't plant a church for its own sake. Instead, churches
should be planted to build the Kingdom of God. The life of
a church must not be self-centred, inward-focussed. Rather,
everything a church is and does, should be subject to the
Lordship of God the King. If that's not the case, the church loses
its purposes and church planting becomes a meaningless exercise.[4]

Consider this example: It's Saturday morning. You leave your apartment and go to the bakery. Once there, you order some bread and rolls. They reply, 'We don't carry bread any more.' And you think to yourself, 'This bakery has a problem.' Or, you go to the local car dealership and want to buy a new car. But the salesman says, 'We have no cars for sale.' You think to yourself, 'This car dealership has a problem.' Or, you go to one of the games of your favourite soccer team. The team is strong defensively, but in the last ten matches they haven't scored a single goal. You think to yourself, 'My team has a problem.' When the bakery doesn't bake bread and the car dealership doesn't sell cars and the soccer team never scores a goal, there are big problems.

It's Monday morning. You stop by to visit a friend. He tells you all the time that he's a Christian. But when you look at his life, there's very little to differentiate it from the lives of your non-Christian friends. 'What's the big deal?' he asks. 'The main thing is that I believe in Jesus Christ as my Lord and Saviour.' And that's just it: many professing Christians don't seem to be bothered by the fact that no one can tell they are Christians.

In the first century, Jews looked to the Torah and to particularly pious people like the scribes (or teachers of the law) and the Pharisees. They were the measuring rod for spiritual life. The scribes were the men who dedicated themselves to the Scriptures and their meaning. If people had questions about the Scriptures, they went to the scribes for an answer. The Pharisees (or the 'separated ones') were members of an exclusive fellowship of laymen, who were led by the scribes. They agreed on joining the fellowship to strictly observe the tithe and all the regulations governing

---

4 Reimer, p 147.

purity and ritual cleanliness. They wanted to represent the purest form of God's people, and so they separated themselves from the rest of the population, who were common and unclean. The scribes considered themselves to be smarter than everyone else when it came to the Scriptures, and the Pharisees considered themselves better than everyone else because of their strict way of life. Everybody knew that they could not measure up to the scribes or the Pharisees. Those men were simply too good.

With this as a background, the statement of Jesus in Matthew 5:20 is all the more astonishing: 'Unless your righteousness exceeds that of the scribes and Pharisees, you will never enter the kingdom of heaven.' (NRSV, Anglicized)

Is our righteousness greater than that of the scribes and Pharisees? Does our life have a special quality that the life of the religious elite in Jesus' day did not have?

The Shop-Window Religion of the Scribes and Pharisees

In Matthew 23, Jesus takes the religious elite to task. He says, 'They do all their deeds to be seen by others'. Their good deeds were not the problem; it was their motivation that was the problem. They wanted recognition. Their prayer shawls and tassels were size XXL; they sat in the best seats in the synagogue; they all wanted to be called Rabbi or Teacher.

In 1970, when I was 12 years old, my family and I visited West Berlin, where we had relatives. One day Uncle Heinz took us on a drive through the city. At one point, next to a row of houses, we parked the car and walked along the pavement. It seemed to me to be an ordinary street. The row of houses had curtains in the windows, flower boxes, doors and mailboxes. But then I looked more closely. What I noticed startled me. Behind the windows, there was a solid wall. We climbed up a tower that was standing in the street and from there I could see that the entire row of houses was only a façade. Behind the façade was a wall, and behind the wall was an empty minefield, and behind that lay East Berlin. The row of houses was nothing more than whitewash.

Some people live a shop-window religion. Outwardly everything looks fine: they are decent people, helpful, reliable. But what hides behind the façade is empty and lifeless. Paul calls this 'self-imposed piety' (Colossians 2:23, NRSV, Anglicized). It is the result of a life governed by human-made rules. It makes people feel good about themselves, and they assume others think well of them. But they are no more than play-actors who resemble the (lost) elder brother in Jesus' parable of the prodigal son. He appeared to be a well-behaved member of the family, but he lacked a heart-felt relationship with his father (Luke 15:28–30).

To live a life of self-righteousness turns out to be very, very stressful. You have to always be in control of yourself, so that everything works out as you want it to. You have to ensure that everyone around you approves of you. And all of this has to happen in your own strength, which is neither easy nor fun. It's hard work.

'For I tell you, unless your righteousness exceeds that of the scribes and Pharisees, you will never enter the kingdom of heaven' (Matthew 5:20).

Righteousness Better than that of the Scribes and Pharisees

To live more righteousnessly than the scribes and Pharisees is not possible through greater effort or better performance. Instead, it refers to a different kind of living, which draws from another source: the Lord Jesus, who through his lordship frees us to live righteously. The difference between the two is as great as the difference between day and night.

A righteousness that is given to us

What must we do in order to be accepted by God and admitted into fellowship with him? The answer to this question brings us very close to the righteousness of the scribes and Pharisees. Because as soon as we think that we have to do something to win God's favour, we are thinking just like the Pharisees did.

The Sermon on the Mount is held in high esteem by many intellectuals because of its moral clarity. Many see in the Sermon on the Mount a political strategy. But the Sermon on the Mount cannot be experienced without focussing on the sermon-giver, Jesus. Jesus said, 'Do not think I have come to abolish the law or the prophets; I have come not to abolish but to fulfil' (Matthew 5:17).

Jesus satisfied the demands of the Old Testament law, something that no other person, not even a Pharisee, had ever been able to do. The message of the Sermon on the Mount and the entire New Testament is that regular, flawed human beings, who constantly fail, can be righteous before God – but only as a gift of God. Jesus fulfilled the demands of the law that we can never fulfil. Jesus, who died on the cross, paid the debt of our sin. Forgiveness and reconciliation with God the Father is always a gift. Righteousness can never be self-righteousness; no one can make himself righteous in God's eyes.

The Apostle Paul said it well: 'There is no distinction, since all have sinned and fall short of the glory of God; they are now justified by his grace as a gift, through the redemption that is in Christ Jesus' (Romans 3:23–24, NRSV, Anglicized). What must we do in order to be accepted by God? Nothing! Anyone who has accepted Christ as Lord and Saviour has also received the righteousness of Christ.

When the people who listened to Jesus understood his message, they wanted to be part of God's kingdom, to be recipients of his grace and power, whatever the cost. So at the conclusion of the Sermon of the Mount, we read of a leper who comes to Jesus. He is healed, made clean, and enters the kingdom of God.

A righteousness that is better than that of the scribes and Pharisees is a righteousness that *we* cannot earn. It is a gift. And it is a righteousness that changes our *hearts*. The righteousness of the Pharisees only changed the outside, but not the heart. That was the problem.

A righteousness that changes our hearts

Jesus' gift to us is a new heart – his heart, the heart of God, so much more than behaviour modification. A new orientation penetrates our entire life and becomes noticeable on the outside, too: we've become children of God. Children are shaped by their parents, children of God are shaped by their Father in heaven. They begin to think, feel, and act like him. Mark Twain once said, 'What's the use of training if children end up like their parents anyway!' God's children take on the character of their heavenly Father.

In practice this means more than refraining from murder; it means having the power to refuse to hate, even when we have been hurt. It means more than no longer insulting people who have wronged us; it means the ability to refuse to despise another human being. It means more than not committing adultery; it means the freedom to refrain from desiring any person other than our spouse as partner. It means more than not hating our enemies: it means the capacity to love them. All of this is the new mindset of those who have become citizens of the kingdom of God. It gives a foretaste of what will come. It is heaven on earth in my life.

The prophet Jeremiah painted us a picture of God's future in the lives of his children:

> *'I will put my law within them, and I will write it on their*
> *hearts; and I will be their God, and they shall be my people.*
> *No longer shall they teach one another, or say to each other,*
> *"Know the LORD," for they shall all know me, from the least*
> *to the greatest, says the Lord. I will forgive their iniquity, and*
> *remember their sin no more' (Jeremiah 31:33–34).*

In God's new world, everyone will automatically obey God's commandments. It will be as natural as breathing.

And what is still in the future is already present in Jesus. It means I live as if Jesus lived in my skin, because he lives in my heart. It means I live in the righteousness which is better than the righteousness of the scribes and Pharisees.

One of the prayers that many German parents teach their children has rather bad theology: 'Come, Lord Jesus, be our guest, and may your gifts to us be blessed.' It sounds good but is wrong. If Jesus is our Lord, he can not be our guest. A guest leaves, but the lord of the house stays. That brief prayer is also wrong on another count: it asks Jesus to come. If he can come, then he can also go. Jesus does not want to come and go in our lives. He wants to stay. And when he stays, he stays as Lord of our inner world and our outer world. And he blesses us with a righteousness that we have not earned. He changes our hearts in such a way that over time we begin to think and act like him. Then we experience the future now.

We live in righteousness that is better than the righteousness of the scribes and Pharisees.

Putting into Practice the Liberating Lordship of Christ

If we want to stop living for ourselves and start experiencing how Jesus can liberate us to fulfil his purposes, to live for his glory, then we need some practical steps that will help us.

A heart on fire

'Were not our hearts burning within us while he talked with us…?' (Luke 24:32). We need burning hearts in church-planting work, like the hearts of those disciples on the way to Emmaus. Then there are no limits to where Jesus can lead us. The heart is the control room of a person's life – whoever or whatever rules in her heart will control and direct her.

After a church has been planted and has passed through the first phases of growth, it gets dangerous. In the beginning of a church-planting ministry, it may seem almost effortless to keep our hearts on fire for Jesus. Everything is new and exciting. God is at work. Prayers are being answered. But then things start to become routine; we can start taking them for granted. Busy-ness (a spirit of activism) can set in. Outwardly there may be little noticeable change, but on the inside, in the heart, things could have subtly shifted.

When I was seven years old, my best friend Donald and I unintentionally became arsonists. We were both adventure-seekers and we planned to build a small bonfire on the edge of a wooded area near our homes. As aspiring Boy Scouts, we knew what we were doing. First we built up a circle of stones. Then we gathered straw and branches and piled them up carefully. Then we lit a match and stepped back to watch. We were rewarded with a briskly burning fire. But we soon noticed that we had too much of a good thing. The flames reached higher and higher. Our little stone circle was completely ineffective as a containment wall. It was time for damage control! We found an old bucket and drew water from a nearby stream to throw on the fire. But the bucket was rusted and leaked badly. We quickly lost water, and then hope. The only thing we could think to do was to crawl on all fours through grain fields in order to get home without being seen. We hoped the fire would burn itself out. But it didn't. The fire department was called. The police came and talked with the neighbours. Terrified by the sight of the policemen in their uniforms with brightly polished badges, we broke down in tears. Busted!

The woods near my home were almost completely destroyed by that fire. There was plenty of fuel for the fire right there all around our little bonfire. Once Jesus has come with his love and grace and set our hearts on fire, we have to make sure a sufficient supply of fuel exists to keep the fire going. What keeps the fire burning is surely different from one disciple to the next. God's word has to be part of the fuel for each of us. The disciples on the way to Emmaus said their hearts were burning, 'while he talked with us on the road and opened the Scriptures to us' (Luke 24:32). The prophet Jeremiah, too, recognized the word of God as fuel. God told him so directly: 'Is not my word like fire ... and like a hammer that breaks a rock in pieces?' (Jeremiah 23:29). When the fire goes out in the heart of a Christian, then it is often a result of insufficient time in the word of God. A daily supply of God's word – whether through a quiet time, a spiritual book or a devotional reading on the internet – will keep our passion for Jesus burning brightly. Memorizing passages of Scripture is a way of storing God's word in our hearts, so that we can recall it and flame it into fire.

A clean conscience

Isn't it a little strange how Jesus sometimes dealt with people who had physical disabilities? Remember the story of the man who had to be carried on a stretcher by his friends because he was unable to walk (Mark 2), or the story of the man who had been crippled and had been lying by a pool for 38 years (John 5)? Before Jesus healed these men physically so that they could walk again, he first addressed the condition of their hearts. He forgave them their sins before he healed them. For Jesus, the broken relationship with God because of unforgiven sin was a much deeper problem for these men than their physical disabilities. Matthew 18 informs us that Jesus assumes that there will be sin within the fellowship of believers. So he gives us clear instructions about how to resolve conflict and be reconciled with one another. Because we want to win the person who has sinned against us

(Matthew 18:15), we go to him and talk about it in private, just between the two of us. If that doesn't resolve things, we are told to take a trusted person with us as witness. Only if this step fails as well are we to bring the problem before the church.

Sin that is unconfessed and not dealt with in the life of a Christ-follower affects his spiritual life like the emptying of a bucket of water over a bonfire: all spiritual passion is extinquished. When sin is tolerated in a church, prayers become hollow, testimonies of God's activity become powerless, and the atmosphere becomes cold.

I meet regularly with a Christian friend. We ask one another how we're doing. We ask tough questions. Confessing my sins to this brother and to God does me a world of good. Think of it as letting fresh air into a room that has been closed up for too long and smells musty. Open all the windows. Let the fresh air pour in. I leave these conversations feeling light and free. Honest confession, acknowledging where our behaviour or our thoughts have fallen short in God's eyes, serves to fan the fires of our heart back into flame.

Applied listening

People who heard and loved Jesus, wanted to obey his words. In the Christian life our relationship with Christ and all the goodness that we experience through him awakens in us the desire to love him by obeying him. To respond in any other way to him and his word is insulting. The test of whether we have heard him in his word is obedience. At the conclusion of the Sermon on the Mount, Jesus turns to his audience and talks about their response to his words. He divides his audience into two groups: the ones who understood what he said, but chose not to act accordingly, and the ones who heard and acted (Matthew 7:24). In order to keep our hearts on fire, we have to read the Bible with the attitude: 'Lord, whatever you show me in your word, I will do.'

If we want to keep our hearts burning for Jesus, then we must be real with God and with ourselves. What does it mean to be real? We are real when we are what we seem to be, when what we are on the outside, what other people can see in our behaviour, is what we are on the inside.

Jesus directed harsh criticism against religious leaders who were not real. 'Woe to you, scribes and Pharisees, hypocrites! For you clean the outside of the cup and of the plate, but inside they are full of greed and self-indulgence' (Matthew 23:25, NRSV, Anglicized). It is hypocrisy when the reality of who we are on the inside (how we think and how we are) is different from the image we present on the outside.

To be real means: 'I am in fact myself. What I say and what I do are not contradictory.' I do things from my heart. I do them willingly, gladly, unforced, in an uncontrived way. Then I am real. Helmut Thielicke wrote, 'Just as I am fully present in my actions, thus I am real, so too the Lord is also truly fully present in him [my neighbour]. Because *He* is, of course, the one who meets me in the hungry, the imprisoned, the thirsty, the homeless (Matthew 25:35ff); Jesus walks the earth in the disguise of my neighbour.'[5] In following Christ, the Christian becomes increasingly like Christ. In this way she lives out her true identity and is joyful.

I don't know about you, but I sometimes worry that my heart can become cold. The thought of living an unfeeling, passionless, powerless life before God terrifies me. And how fast that can happen! How easy it is to get there. I just stop paying attention to God. I just stay so busy with the tasks of the day that I have no time left for God. Sure, I can still accomplish something. But my heart shrinks and develops cracks. I start promoting 'Ego Ltd'. It should come as no surprise then that my sensitivity to God and others diminishes, that I become moody, irritable, impatient, self-absorbed, unbearable.

I sometimes notice that my heart can become calculating. And I've learned that when my heart starts to be calculating, my fire for Jesus starts to go out. The calculating heart is constantly weighing options, and asks, 'Can I get by if I ignore God right now? What harm will it do anyway if I go my way and allow God only a little bit of room in my life? What good will it do me if I follow God's way in this or that? Probably not much.' Behind every calculating heart there is an expedient, unscrupulous nature. If I let go of reverence for God, I inevitably lose my centre, my anchor. When I lose that centre, then trivialities will move in – my own well-being, my finances, my free time, my possessions. Soon they become a super power that influences everything in my life. When they take the centre stage, they rule my life and assume an importance they should never have.

---

5 Thielicke, p 22.

Based on these trivialities, I decide whether something is advantageous or disadvantageous for me. And my heart grows cold.

But what happens when, as a principle, I say yes to Jesus and to doing his will? I grow in understanding. 'Jesus answered them, "My teaching is not mine but his who sent me. Anyone who resolves to do the will of God will know whether the teaching is from God or whether I am speaking on my own"' (John 7:16–17, NRSV, Anglicized).

Some insights in the life of a disciple come only *after* she has obeyed what God has taught her. We will find that the teaching of the Bible confirms itself: the teaching sounds authentic, and the doing confirms the authenticity of the teaching.

Why is it that some Christians have not had any new insights from God for a long time? Because they have refused to put into practice what they already know. God will not lead us beyond our willingness to obey. Some Christians are bored. The source of their boredom is not God. It is their refusal to pay attention to God's word after he has made it perfectly clear to them what they are to do. When we start obeying Jesus again, we will receive new insights from God.

Too often we are like Jill in the Narnia stories: we're afraid of the Lion. But it's not until we submit to him and his lordship that we can drink from the refreshing stream. Church planters will succeed in planting churches that are oases of God's love if they place themselves and the people they lead under the lordship of Jesus Christ. There, under his leadership, they will find the liberating power that they have longed for, and with which they can build the kingdom of God.

EIGHT

Changed Identity

It is essential that the person who has entered into a relationship with Jesus also allows himself to be changed by Christ. If that does not happen, the whole process of multiplication is at risk.

The Danger of Christian Socialization

Whenever we speak with friends about the greatest dangers to the church of Jesus Christ, we hear a wide range of opinions. 'The greatest danger lies in the increasing secularization of society, which influences the church as well and makes her more and more secular,' say some. Others say, 'No, it's the lack of commitment on the part of church members. Twenty per cent of the church does 80 per cent of the work. If more people got actively involved, our churches would be stronger.' A third voice says, 'The church is most in danger when she's inwardly focussed and isn't living for those outside the church who are not yet believers.' Even if all three of these perspectives contained some truth and represented a danger to the church, none of them describes what is ultimately the greatest threat to the existence of the church. In my opinion, the greatest danger to the church of Jesus Christ – the thing that threatens her existence, saps her strength and robs her of her credibility – is a Christian socialization of her members.

Recently my son, Lukas, and I went to a local jeweller and wanted to exchange some silver. Since I was 12 years old, I have been an active treasure seeker. With a number of different kinds of metal detectors, I'm always looking for old coins and jewellery in my free time. I'm always excited about the treasures I dig up: gold and silver rings, coins of all kinds, jewellery. Admittedly I also dig up a lot of worthless junk, and my family often reminds me of that fact: 'How many beer and cola cans did you find today?' Or, 'Will this make your retirement funds unnecessary?' On the day in question, Lukas and I brought a handful of silver rings, coins, spoons and jewellery to this jeweller and wanted to receive cash in exchange. He looked at my treasures, laid a few things aside, weighed the others, and gave me some money for them (about enough to buy two ice cream cones). 'What about the other pieces?' I asked him. 'They're not genuine,' he said. I thought they were made of sterling silver, but they were simply things that had a silvery lustre.

Christian-looking people are those who have become socialized Christians but who are not genuine. They pose the greatest danger to the church. On many occasions, Jesus warned his followers about this. Even if Jesus' teaching about the kingdom of God cannot be totally applied to the church, similar things happen today in the church, we can be sure. We find people in our church who receive the word of God 'with joy' but who don't stick with it because they have 'no root' (Luke 8:13). Or people who seem to grow as Christians but bear no fruit, because worries, riches and 'the pleasures of life' (Luke 8:14) choke off the fruit. People like these are members and casual attenders of our churches. In Jesus' own ministry, there was an occasion that we read about with sadness when 'Many of his disciples turned back and no longer followed him' (John 6:66). Jesus quoted the prophet Isaiah, who wrote, 'These people honour me with their lips, but their hearts are far from me' (Mark 7:6). Empty rituals, without Jesus at the heart, were the sad reality even among Jesus' listeners. Even among the Twelve, to whom Jesus gave power to work miracles and to preach about the kingdom of God, was one who turned out to be 'a devil': Judas (John 6:70). If Jesus himself knew what it was to have some forsake him, who were once part of his team and who were actively involved in his ministry, we should not be surprised that we are threatened by the same danger.

It's easier than you would think to fall prey to this threat. Anyone who has grown up in a Christian home and views church attendance and Christian ethics as a normal part of his life can be a threat to the church through his involvement. Anyone who bases her self-worth on her accomplishments, whether in her personal life, her work life, or her church life, can be a danger to the church. People who love to be a part of something exciting – like the planting of a new church – and derive their sense of meaning from this, can be dangerous.

Police detectives are taught to recognize counterfeit money. They learn this skill not by studying counterfeit bills, but by becoming very familiar with the real thing. We should follow their example. I do not mean that we should start assessing whether someone in our church is a genuine Christian or not. It's simply important that we learn to recognize the true identity of a Christ-follower, that we teach about it and live it out ourselves.

Being a Child of God Creates Identity

It wasn't until after Jesus' resurrection that people started calling his followers Christians. The term 'Christian' only occurs three times in the Bible (Acts 11:26; 26:28; 1 Peter 4:16) and was originally used derisively. The first Christians did not really know what to make of the term. They thought of themselves as children of God, disciples, and Christ-followers, and it was these concepts that gave them their identity. The terms *disciples* and *followers* are used almost four hundred times in the New Testament to refer to people whose lives were patterned on Jesus'. The Christian environment does not give us our identity, but rather Christ himself, and our own follower-ship.

The Apostle John goes to great efforts in the prologue of his Gospel (John 1:1–14) to make clear that Jesus Christ came from God and was (is) God. John writes about people who 'believed in his [Jesus'] name' (John 1:12). In Judaism, a person's name confirmed his existence. To believe in the name of Jesus means to count on his reality, to know who he is and to entrust oneself to him. Faith in Christ was never something done from a distance. It has always been an expression of a genuine connection to and solidarity with Jesus.

John writes that God gave those who 'believed in his name' power to become 'children of God' (John 1:12). John talks here about personal identity. The Bible tells us that the very first humans were made 'in the image of God' (Genesis 1:26). This speaks of the human understanding of who we are. We received our identity, our awareness of our own existence, and our value from God. We know well enough through the Bible that humankind's rebellion against God resulted in people being separated from God. And although people still retain fragments of God's image (e.g. intelligence, the ability to rule, the capacity to discover and create beauty, to be self-aware), many now live without the original connection to God, without an identity derived from God himself. Therefore, most people, separated from God as they are, seek to acquire or create their own identity.

Being a Christian is different, however. Identity is not acquired but given: 'To all who received him, who believed in his name, he gave power to become children of God' (John 1:12, NRSV, Anglicized). A person becomes a child of God because God makes her his child. We call that grace. Grace is unearned. It is God's gift to us, without our having to do anything, or being able to do anything to earn it.

Jesus taught his disciples that they were children of his Father – children of God. 'Be merciful, just as your Father is merciful' (Luke 6:36). 'Pray then in this way: Our Father in heaven…' (Matthew 6:9, NRSV, Anglicized). The child of God receives the traits of his nature, his self-acceptance, his sense of belonging, from the connection to his heavenly Father.

Even to speak about God as 'Father' was something completely new to Jewish and Greek ears. In the Old Testament God was described as Creator, Judge, Saviour, and Redeemer, but not as Father. Jesus revealed a new aspect when he spoke of God as Father. It's an intimate, affectionate way to think about God. Jesus used the common term 'Abba' for his Father. 'Abba' or 'Papa' or 'Daddy' all stem from early childhood – as is shown by the fact that these words can all be spoken without the use of teeth. The expression 'Abba Father' is saturated with affection, familiarity and security.

For beginners, but also for those more advanced in their faith, the importance of seeing and really taking to heart what a miracle it is that we are made children of God is huge. If, as Jesus said, we must be 'born from above' (John 3:3, NRSV, Anglicized) in order to see the kingdom of God, that involves a new identity. As children of God, our Father in heaven is the origin of our existence. We have received from him a qualitatively new eternal life. He *is* that life, brought to us through Jesus. Because our life originates in the Father, we belong to him. He is responsible for our welfare since we have *become* his children through Jesus. Furthermore, the Father loves us as his children. Martin Luther once said, 'God is like a glowing oven full of love.' We live in the radiant warmth of the love of our Father. And yet many Christians find it difficult to appropriate this unbelievably beautiful truth for themselves – that they each are a child of God.

We love to light candles in our home, especially in the wintertime. When our children were still little, they loved the liquid wax. As soon as the candle wax began to melt, they would shape it however they liked. But they knew they had to work quickly, because as soon as the wax cooled off, they could no longer change its shape.

When children come into the world, they are like liquid wax. Up until five or six years of age, they can be shaped. In this crucial period, their environment plays a decisive role in how they see themselves and thus in the development of their sense of self-worth. A child's self-image is shaped by what is communicated by his parents and teachers. And because a child is not yet capable of differentiating between good and bad influences, he soaks up everything that comes his way. A child adopts the conclusions of others as his own. The opinions of others cling to the child's thinking, and are not easily shed in later life. Why are some adults bent over like a candle that's been in the sun? Because they were shaped like that, and badly, by others during the formative years of their childhood.

The acceptance and security that may have been missing in our childhood can be supplied by our Father in heaven. Healing happens through the connection to Jesus, since Jesus connects us to God our Father (John 14:6). Once we have come to the Father, we learn to think differently and to see ourselves as he sees us. We learn to accept that he has made us his children and that he loves us. His love is unconditional and indestructible. Many adults still long for this kind of love from their parents. Yet what parents may have failed to give us, our heavenly Father gladly gives.

Let us not overlook the pronoun that comes before the word 'Father' in the Lord's Prayer. Note the word 'our'. Not I alone am a child of God. The church is the family of God, and I am 'related' to others who have also been given the gift of being children of God. It is unnatural for a follower of Jesus to try and follow him on her own. Jesus did not have this in mind. When he calls us to himself, he also calls us to one another and for one another.

Making People Disciples

Our new identity which Jesus gives us is anchored in the Trinity. We read in the Great Commission that Jesus said to his followers, 'All authority in heaven and on earth has been given to me. Therefore go and make disciples of all nations, baptizing them in the name of the Father and of the Son and of the Holy Spirit, and teaching them to obey everything I have commanded you' (Matthew 28:18–20). The main responsibility we are given is found in the phrase 'make disciples'. Make out of people, who are living for themselves or who are living for other people or other purposes, *my* disciples, i.e., students, trainees, apprentices of Jesus. How do we do that?

Jesus tells us that two things are important if people are to become disciples: immersion and application. In this context, application means that people learn how to 'obey' Jesus' teaching, and how to apply it in their everyday lives. If people understand what Jesus said, but do not know how to apply it in their lives, real teaching has not happened. Teaching without application is meaningless. The goal is not the transfer of information but the transformation of lives.

But the first thing that Jesus says about his new disciples is that we should immerse people into the reality of the Triune God, which is more than baptism. Baptism presupposes that the one being baptized has already, before her baptism, been immersed into the reality of God. We have already discovered that the 'name' of a person is connected to the reality of the person who bears the name. In baptism, a person is immersed and surrounded by water. In the same way, a disciple is immersed in God the Father, Son, and Holy Spirit. A disciple turns from his world as the reliable reality, and discovers that he participates in the reality of God himself. The new environment of his life consists of his relationship to the Triune God. He has found in God the Father, Son, and Holy Spirit a new meaning – he belongs to God. His identity is now in God. This baptism is not, like that of John the Baptist, a baptism of repentance (Matthew 11:12). It is rather a baptism *into* (Greek, *eis*) fellowship with the Triune God.

There is no other life as beautiful and as challenging as the life of a follower of Jesus Christ. To follow Christ is to enrol in the school of life where God designs the curriculum individually for each of his children.

Jesus is the Lord. The disciples are his students, his followers, and they are the body of Christ in training. Jesus loves his Father above all else; Jesus' followers learn what it means to love the Father in heaven more than anything else. Jesus served other people devotedly and joyfully; Jesus' followers learn what it means to serve others joyfully and sacrificially. But why should someone who has begun to believe in Jesus start to align her life with Jesus' life? The answer to this question has to do with a person's identity. Anyone who has trusted Christ and has begun to walk with him and to orient her life around him, discovers her own true identity. She knows who she really is.

The Collective Identity of the Church

As individuals who are following Jesus, we should draw our identity from God and live consistent with that identity. Especially at the start of a new church, keep in mind that this new identity has a collective dimension as well. This affects four areas of our life together: our future, our mission, our power source, and our impact on society.

Christ-followers have a preferred future *together*. When Jesus comes again, the angels will gather in Jesus' elect (Mark 13:27; cf. John 14:3). Jesus' followers will see his glory with their own eyes and no longer simply with the eyes of faith (John 17:24). In Jesus' new world his disciples will have homes (John 14:2). Along with countless other followers of Jesus, after the resurrection we will live with God forever in the indestructible power of a new life (John 11:25).

And *together*, Jesus' followers are sent out into the harvest field (Matthew 9:37–38). Here and now we have a common mission in the world: 'Make disciples of all nations' (Matthew 28:19). The verb form is plural. It is not a commission given to a few specialists or to individual Christians with particular training. This is a commission that is given to every Christian in every church in every generation. Together, collectively, the church makes Christ known, teaches people how to live with Jesus and how to reach others for Christ.

Together a church learns what it means to experience Jesus as her source of nourishment and power. Without 'eating' and 'drinking' Christ, a church will never have the strength to live with God's authority. It is only possible through Jesus, and only together through Jesus. A young church will want to find ways to come together to worship the Father and the Son, and to ask God to work in their lives to accomplish their sanctification and to work miracles of healing. Dallas Willard once said that he would never accept a call to a church that was not willing to follow a Bible memory plan. Churches can learn together to inhale generous amounts of oxygen (God's word) so that they stay healthy.

When we memorize God's word, it colours our soul – both the soul of individual Christians as well as the soul of an entire church. 'Let the word of Christ *dwell* in you richly' (Colossians 3:16, NRSV, Anglicized). We can picture a fruit tree that even during times of drought is healthy and loaded with life-giving fruit (Psalm 1:3). Memorizing passages of Scripture together as a church should be a normal part of church life. When it is, it promotes a congregation's spiritual well-being and its healthy, effective ministry in the community.

The life of a church should not only be evangelistic and missional. The collective life of a church should also be a blessing to society. Jesus likened his team to a city on a hill that shines its light on the people all around (Matthew 5:14). A church should be noticed by the community around them. It should be recognized by non-Christians for the added value it brings to that community through its deeds of love, justice and service: 'that they may see your good works and give glory to your Father in heaven' (Matthew 5:16, NRSV, Anglicized).

Small Groups as Places of New Identity

In newly planted churches and in well-established congregations as well, we need places where Christians can live out their new identity in Christ and where others can be invited to experience this new identity. Small groups (cells) of Christians in fellowship with one another can be such places. How vital that new church plants develop a small-group structure so that people's new identity in Christ can be lived out together.

I was 15 years old when I became a Christian and aligned my life with Jesus. Not long after my conversion, I began attending a small group made up of others who were about my age. For almost four decades now I have been an active part of all kinds of small groups, as a participant and as a leader. Many of these groups were very influential in my life. Some were not. I would not recommend doing away with small groups (home groups, cell groups, or whatever they may be called), but I would recommend re-envisioning them so that participants can discover and live out their new identity that is to be found in Christ.

When I was growing up, my family regularly spent time with boats on the water during the summer. A motor boat or a row boat was always involved. My father taught me to row; I learned to sit with my back to the bow and my face to the stern. That positioned me to give the boat its strongest forward motion. And it illustrates a principle: to look to the past, to the many hours spent in small groups, provides perspective that gives strong forward momentum into the future. In order to create more effective small groups in the future, we have to learn from the past and make intentional changes.

The way many small groups are now

Careful reflection on the overall landscape of small groups in the churches I have known, brings me to the following conclusions:

1. The communication of biblical information does not usually lead to personal transformation (change). Despite this fact, most small groups focus primarily on communicating content.
2. Small-group leaders are active; small-group participants, however, tend to be passive.
3. Small group leaders think of themselves as teachers; participants think of themselves as learners.
4. Evangelism rarely, if ever, happens in small groups.
5. Integrating new participants into well-established small groups seldom succeeds.
6. Small groups don't know why they exist, therefore expectations are unclear.
7. The idea of dividing an established group (to give birth to a new group) arouses opposition.

8. The fear of self-disclosure grows proportionally with the size of the small group. A group of 10–12 members (or more) becomes impersonal.

9. The terms 'small group' and 'small-group leader' do not have much meaning. We need new labels.

Keeping sight of the goal

'If you don't know the destination, you can't make the journey. If you don't make the journey, you won't reach the destination.'[1] What is the goal of our human existence? Jesus was asked this same question from a religious perspective: 'Teacher, which is the greatest commandment in the law?' Christ answered: 'Love the Lord your God with all your heart and with all your soul and with all your mind … Love your neighbour as yourself' (Matthew 22:37–39).

Love indicates proximity. Love for God is expressed in a person's devotion to God and consists of experiencing community with him. Love is Jesus' goal for his church, love for God but also love for one another. Only through love can the church make disciples of the nations, by being like Jesus in his hunger to be close to the Father and in his commitment to do the Father's will. What do we often lack?

> *If we do not have a positive relationship with ourselves and do not experience close relationships with others daily (especially spouse and children), we should not be surprised that we do not feel close to someone whom we cannot see, touch, or hear! God is there, and we can experience His presence. But if we have no close relationships on the human level, it is difficult to imagine that we will experience them on a spiritual level.*[2]

Close human relationships open the door for a greater intimacy with God. Seen the other way, a sense that God is distant often derives from the inability to build intimacy and openness with other people. Is it

---

1 Friso Melzer, on the word 'goal' (German, *Ziel*) in February 2013 at: http://www.alfa-coburg.falk-it.de/alfaphp/include.php?path=content/overview.php&type=1&catid=6&letter=&entries=0&searchtext=&order=titled

2 Christopher McCluskey, quoted by Collins, p 228.

possible that in our small groups we are so focussed on wanting to build a relationship with God that we neglect to build relationships with each other? Can it be that our small groups suffer from a lack of closeness among the participants? And that this lack cannot be eliminated by more Bible study and discussion? I strongly suspect that there is an important insight to be gained here.

Changes needed

We are keeping sight of the goal: people living in a close, loving relationship with their heavenly Father and in the safety of warm, open, affectionate relationships with one another. What they experience is almost indescribable: they can be open and vulnerable with others; they know they are liked and accepted; they feel loved. Because of this, they grow in their openness to and love for God. The one leads to the other. How can we make this happen in our small groups? Here are some suggestions:

- The small-group leader changes how he sees himself. He is no longer the teacher but rather a companion in a spiritual process. He uses material that is available to all (questions drawn from the sermon or other available material) instead of preparing everything himself. He is the guardian of the covenant, the shepherd of the group, and the time-keeper.
- A small group covenant exists that everyone knows and accepts. The covenant contains mutually agreed upon statements of the goal(s) of the group, the structure of the meetings, the requirements for the participants, the meeting day, time and frequency, the length of meetings, and so on. Participation in the covenant is by invitation only.
- Within a small group there are committed mini-groups. Half of the meeting time consists of an open and honest discussion among gender-specific mini-groups of three or four members. A supplied list of questions forms the basis of discussion for these mini-groups which function without a designated leader.

10 minutes	45 minutes	35 minutes
Worship	**Gender-specific mini groups**	**Bible study/discussion**

Figure 7: Proposed structure of a small-group meeting (90 minutes)

The strengths of mini groups

Mini groups need no leader. Because of the small size, a high level of trust can be built. It is possible in an atmosphere like this to practice mutual accountability concerning the events of the week. People can talk about what they have (or haven't) experienced with God. Spiritual disciplines can also be practiced here.

Strong structures

We need a structure for our small groups that is stronger than the people in the group. Too often the quality of our small groups is dependent on the personality, maturity, insights and preparation of the leaders. Even the expressed desire to train apprentice leaders can intimidate participants.

In the new structure I propose here, it is possible to minimize a leader's preparation time, to deepen the relationships among the participants, and to further everyone's growth in their love for God. The difference between the old and new ways of forming small groups is like the difference between a standard screwdriver and a power screwdriver: greater efficiency (more love for God and for one another) with less effort.

Regular Small-Group Structure	vs	Proposed New Small-Group Structure
Leadership		Companionship
Significant preparation time		Minimal preparation time
Minimal involvement of participants		High involvement of participants
Large groups		Mini groups
Information		Transformation
Limited openness, minimal self-disclosure		High level of openness, vulnerability, and self-disclosure
'Whoever wants to, can come'		'By invitation only'
120 minutes		90 minutes

Figure 8: Two ways of structuring a small group

In our post-modern society, people are searching for authentic and reliable relationships with others who will offer them acceptance and respect. They long for this because it was often painfully lacking in their family of origin. The church of Jesus should demonstrate healthy inter-personal relationships in a way that offers a positive contrast to what many people have experienced. Citizens of our post-modern society should be able to find authenticity, love, warmth, meaning and identity in the church of Jesus Christ.

NINE

Practical Discipleship

In a Christian institution for the homeless, the employees regularly held worship services for their guests, most of whom were alcoholics. Joe was an employee. Harry was a guest. He had no family and no regular employment. His life was so out of control that everyone had abandoned him: his wife, his children, his employer, his friends – everyone but Joe. Joe was someone he could talk to. Joe picked up Harry off the streets each night, made sure he had a bath, something to eat and a warm bed. Harry found in Joe a friend who would stick with him through thick and thin. Everyone else had given him up as a hopeless case, but Joe would not turn his back on Harry.

Harry had heard many sermons there. But on this particular occasion, the message went straight to his heart. At the end of the service, Harry hobbled to the front, where he made a very important decision. The preacher asked him if he wanted to put his faith in Jesus. 'Is Jesus like Joe?' Harry asked. 'If Jesus is like Joe, I want to entrust my life to him.'

To transform a society through the planting of thousands of new churches, we need to train and empower thousands of new disciples of Jesus called 'Joe', so that from this pool of disciples, who have been tested in real life, a new generation of leaders may come who are able to join and motivate others to plant new churches. The foundation for spiritual leadership is spiritual discipleship; the secret of good leadership is practical discipleship.

Developing Disciples who Lead

The church needs more than conversions. The church needs disciples. Jesus called people to follow him. Those who were with him, observed him and were placed in the service of the kingdom of God as they applied Jesus' teaching in their lives and grew to be more like him. Only after Jesus was convinced of their faithful discipleship (follower-ship) was he able to transfer leadership to them.

This chapter introduces a radical re-thinking of leadership training. I propose that the basis for good leadership is becoming a good apprentice (disciple) of Jesus. But we will begin at the beginning and try to pose a question that has not been asked so far: Is there a self-multiplying way to train new leaders?

After more than twenty years of church planting ministry, during which time five churches were established and continue to grow, I feel a deep sense of gratitude, without being fully satisfied with the results of my ministry. However, I am more convinced than ever that we have to move from planting new churches by 'addition' to planting new churches by 'multiplication'. That means we need to empower young, growing disciples to produce other disciples, which is what I call 'multiplication'.

Culturally-relevant church planting differs from traditional church planting. Culturally-relevant churches have an abundance of motivated leaders, a focus on small groups, exciting and relevant worship services, a relatively homogenous age structure, and a functional method for reaping a spiritual harvest. New converts are placed in their own small groups, discover their identity in Christ and are taught to reach out to their non-Christian friends. In these churches, sincere, involved people who devotedly work to spread the kingdom of God, see that happen. The church is a centre of productive ministry that is not dependent on the influence of a single leader, but instead there exists a system that continually mobilizes and empowers new leaders. Volunteers feel supported and are encouraged to train others, even while they find themselves in an ongoing community of learners, where, for example, they are learning to identify their gifts and to use them. In addition, a coaching system for leaders is established. As far as leadership development goes – which is the focal point of this different, culturally-relevant way of church planting – the traditional way of training leaders must be replaced with a more 'apostolic' training process, as summarized in the following table.

Traditional Leadership Development	vs	'Apostolic' Leadership Development
Intuition		Assignment
Addition		Multiplication
Complex		Simple
Instruction		Training by doing
Front-end learning (theoretical)		Learning what's next
Regurgitation		Individual coaching
Goal: Quality of the leader		Goal: Quality of the process
Arbitrariness in selection		Reliable yet individual reproduction

Figure 9: Two approaches to leadership development

The leadership that results from traditional methods of leader development is inadequate to unleash a new wave of churches. Only in relatively few cases have those methods produced suitable leaders, and in even fewer cases were those leaders able to develop other leaders. Why is that?

Because most of the time the primary leaders of existing churches use their intuition to identify potential new leaders, they have a good feel for people and for situations that helps them know how to draw others into leadership. But intuition and 'feel' are not reproducible. The real limitation of the traditional method of leadership development is this: new leaders may be added, but they will not be multiplied. Intuition is subjective – I choose who I like. Reproduction is objective – I can train anyone to do the things I have learned to do. Traditional leadership development in church is also often linked to the effectiveness, or needs, of a ministry rather than to the development of the leaders themselves – the commissioning of new leaders so often depends on the ministry needs at the time. This misses the goal of finding leaders who can influence others. The usual thinking is that only those who have attained a high level of spiritual maturity can become leaders. This makes the pool of suitable candidates very small indeed. The idea that leadership development begins in the spiritual harvest and leads, in turn, back to the harvest field is completely unknown. Furthermore, there is no on-going system to develop new leaders, and when leaders are raised up at all from within the ranks of the church, it happens rather arbitrarily. When churches *have* thought about finding new leaders, the focus has been on those who are in Bible school or have theological training, and not on identifying people with the ability to develop additional new leaders.

I view leadership as 'influence', and it involves two parties: one who is being influenced, and one who exercises influence. In addition, the one doing the influencing shapes the one being influenced in such a way that she can, in turn, influence others. In the kingdom of God, a leader is someone who influences others to love God and their neighbour. Every disciple who takes initiative exercises leadership. The process of training disciples who take initiative then becomes the model for training at all levels of leadership in a supportive, self-reproducing spiritual system – in the system I propose, there are four levels of training.

I have used the letter 'M', the first letter of the word 'model', to visualize how the training process works. The two halves of the 'M' represents the two activities involved in leadership: being influenced, and influencing. Only when the two halves overlap in the middle does the 'M' make sense.

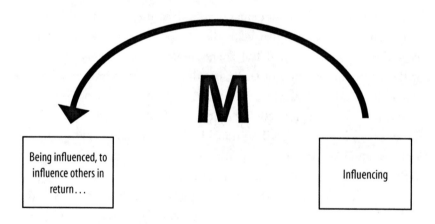

Figure 10: How leadership works in the 'M' model

The Four Phases of the 'M' Model at each Level of Leadership

In my four-phase model of training, the direct influence of the original leader or trainer weakens with each phase. On the other hand, the ones who are being influenced play an increasingly active role in leadership from one phase to the next. The following diagram shows how the 'M' model of training serves as template for developing all four levels of leadership: disciples, coaches, ministry-area leaders and church planters. Each phase of training at each level of leadership serves as a platform for growth to the next.

Training Level (below) or Phase (right)	Phase 1	Phase 2	Phase 3	Phase 4
Disciples	M	M	M	M
Coaches	M	M	M	M
Ministry-Area Leaders	M	M	M	M
Church Planters	M	M	M	M

Figure 11: The four-phase multiplication of leaders at four levels

Imagine that during the training process the right side of the 'M' – the side that exerts influence – slides to the left and then slowly back. Every time an 'M' is complete, a new training process is set in motion.

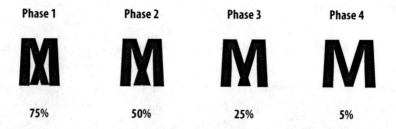

Figure 12: The influence of the trainer in leadership development

The training programme that I outline on the following pages has a '2 x 4' orientation. The '2' represents the two sides of the 'M' – one exercising influence and one being influenced. The '4' represents the four phases of training at each level, as well as the four levels of leadership – disciples, coaches, ministry-area leaders and church planters. At each level, the four-phase training process works in a similar way so that the trainer carries a decreasing responsibility from one phase to the next: from 75 per cent in phase 1 to 5 per cent in phase 4.

Level 1: DISCIPLES

Jesus' Great Commission to go into all the world and 'make disciples' confronts us with the challenge of creating a biblically-based, reproducible system of teaching, so that people will be able to 'obey everything', just as Jesus commanded. Jesus wanted his teaching to be lived out in everyday life. Disciples who are trained with this in mind are able to train others: the product of discipleship is not simply a disciple, but a disciple who produces another disciple. Disciples of Jesus should experience discipleship training in such a way that they not only make progress in their own faith journey but also learn to train others to be disciples of Jesus. Then, at the same time that they are learning from Jesus, they are already in the process of training others to be disciples.

In actual practice, we start with a first group of participants – Christ-followers who want to be trained as disciples. We can begin with two gender-specific groups with three to four Christians in each group. The trainer or primary leader meets with both groups for an entire weekend once every two months over a period of eight months.

Each of these weekends focusses on three key areas which disciples have to master to become trainers of other disciples: orientation – experience – learning.

Most of us were trained at school in a way that somewhat reversed this sequence. We probably received orientation first, followed by learning, and only then experience. Such training is based on the principle that the one who has a lot of knowledge has learned a lot. But has learning occurred if the student has had no opportunity to apply the content in real-life situations? Craig Ott raises this concern and goes on to plead for an experiential approach to learning in our churches, guided by a mentor. The mentor serves as a model and as a trainer. Learning is then measured by how the student uses his abilities in real-life situations.[1]

In order to ensure that the training succeeds, it is important to select the right people to participate. The deciding criteria are an obvious love for God and the desire to grow, willingness to learn and the ability to work with others. Participants must also have the necessary time available to invest in their training. So, how can we, right from the outset of a church-planting project, ensure that people are effectively trained as disciples, coaches, ministry leaders and church planters? The following pages give outlines of a detailed, doable plan to accomplish this.

---

1 Ott, pp 46–50.

Phase 1 of disciple training in mentoring

- Place: a nearby retreat centre
- Time: Friday to Saturday afternoon
- Participants: 3–4 men, 3–4 women, a trainer, a number of volunteer student disciples equal to the number of participants
- Topics: orientation, implementation of a disciple-making experience
- Goal: train Christians how to train others as disciples and empower them
- Material: flip chart, marker, printed copies of the Transformation Flow Chart[2] as handouts for the participants

Friday evening: Participants practice active listening. After a basic introduction, participants are divided into groups of three or four. Taking turns, one person talks about her childhood, a second person is the listener, and the third person is the observer. Note that in this exercise the listener should be able to reflect the content and the emotions of the speaker in his own words. The exercise lasts three minutes per participant. The observer keeps time.

Later in the evening one of the participants is selected by the trainer and together these two demonstrate the disciple-making process for the rest of the group. They discuss the following questions: How are you? What is God teaching you in your Bible reading? What progress are you able to observe in your own discipleship? What obstacles hinder your progress? Who do you know who needs to hear about Jesus, and what role can you play? Do you sense that Jesus wants to change you in any area of your life? What changes do you want to make before our next weekend together? How can I pray for you? Afterwards the group talks about the process that was demonstrated. Questions are asked and problems discussed.

Saturday morning: The trainer explains that a disciple of Jesus needs three things: character, skills and knowledge. On a flip chart the participants list items under each of these headings that a mature

---

2 See Appendix D.

disciple of Christ should possess. Then the trainer explains that the Holy Spirit is the power source throughout the entire discipleship process and that disciples pay attention to his leading. Sanctification, after all, is not linear but is more like a mosaic.

The Transformation Flow Chart is handed out to the participants to help them in their discipleship progress. Participants, in groups of three, practice the use of the Flow Chart.

Lunch

Saturday afternoon: The trainer asks the participants what they have learned thus far about the process of making disciples. Responses are recorded on the flip chart. Final questions are answered.

Coffee Break: During the coffee break, some volunteer student disciples join the group. These are people who have agreed ahead of time to enter into a disciple-making relationship with one of the participants. After the coffee break the first conversations, based on the Transformation Flow Chart, take place between the new participant mentors and the volunteer student disciples with whom they have just been paired.

Homework: During the next eight weeks, the participant mentors meet each week with their student disciples.

Two months pass.

Phase 2 of disciple training in mentoring

- Place: a nearby retreat centre
- Time: Friday evening to Saturday afternoon
- Participants: 3–4 men, 3–4 women, a trainer
- Topics: experience coaching, learn how to coach, practice coaching
- Goal: to learn results-oriented coaching and practice the skills involved
- Material: flip chart, marker, books (*Coaching 101: Discover the Power of Coaching*, by Robert E. Logan and Sherilyn Carlton; *Celebration of Discipline: The Path to Spiritual Growth* by Richard Foster; *Too Busy Not to Pray* by Bill Hybels; printed copies of the P³O³ Model for Coaching[3])

Friday evening: After a time of worship and prayer, the trainer asks the participant mentors to talk about their mentoring experience with their student disciples in the intervening time since the weekend two months earlier – what they can celebrate, what problems they have encountered, and what they have learned.

While the group looks on, the trainer then coaches one of the participants based on the P³O³ model of coaching. Afterwards, the trainer asks the group for their observations about coaching. The one being coached talks about how it felt for her. Comments and results are recorded on the flip chart.

Saturday morning: The trainer leads the participants through the four basic points of effective coaching according to Logan and Carlton: reporting, reflecting, re-concentrating, and resource discovery. Participants are given a copy of *Coaching 101*.

Lunch

Saturday afternoon: The participant mentors discuss what they have experienced thus far as well as the strengths of coaching. In the coming eight weeks the participant mentors will continue their mentoring with their student disciples. During this time the

---

3 See Fig 13 on p 146.

participant mentors will receive two coaching sessions from the trainer.

Coffee Break and Conclusion

Homework: In preparation for the next phase, participant mentors are given two books to read: *Celebration of Discipline* and *Too Busy Not to Pray*. Each participant mentor is asked to choose one spiritual discipline he plans to practice over the next two months, and to write a short description he will use to explain this discipline to the group at the next meeting.

Two months pass.

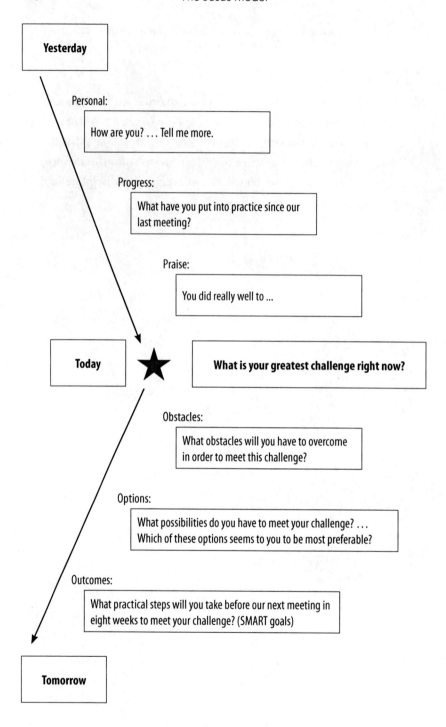

Figure 13: The P³O³ model for coaching

Phase 3 of disciple training in mentoring

- Place: a nearby retreat centre
- Time: Saturday
- Participants: 3–4 men, 3–4 women, a trainer
- Topic: spiritual disciplines
- Goal: get to know new spiritual disciplines, teach them, and experience a learning community
- Material: flip chart, marker, books (*Celebration of Discipline*, Foster; *Too Busy Not to Pray*, Hybels)

Saturday morning: After a time of worship and prayer, the trainer asks the participant mentors to report on their mentoring experience with their student disciples, and on their own coaching sessions. Gathered in groups of three, each participant mentor is asked to describe problems encountered in training their student disciples. The other participant mentors in the group seek to provide coaching based on the P^{3}O^3 model. Results are reported to the whole group.

Lunch

Saturday afternoon: In groups of three, each participant describes a spiritual discipline to the other two.

Homework: Before the next meeting, each participant is asked to practice an additional spiritual discipline which they will report back to the others at the next meeting. The participant mentors continue mentoring their student disciples and each receives two further coaching sessions from the trainer.

Two months pass.

Phase 4 of disciple training in mentoring

- Place: a nearby retreat centre
- Time: Saturday
- Participants: 3–4 men, 3–4 women, a trainer
- Topic: spiritual disciplines
- Goal: a deeper understanding and experience of spiritual disciplines
- Material: flip chart, marker, books (*Celebration of Discipline*, Foster; *Too Busy Not to Pray*, Hybels)

Saturday morning: After a time of worship and prayer, the trainer asks the participant mentors to talk about their experience with their student disciples and about their coaching sessions, as well as their practice of spiritual disciplines. Results are captured on the flip chart.

The participants gather in their groups of three in which they teach one another about the spiritual disciplines they have practiced. Afterwards there is a time of discussion with the entire group. This phase ends with a time of prayer, thanksgiving and praise to God, followed by *Lectio Divina*.[4] Afterwards the entire group celebrates with a delicious meal.

Homework: The participant mentors are encouraged to ask volunteer student disciples who have completed the mentoring experience, to register for the next cycle of disciple training. In addition, each participant mentor who has completed the four phases is invited to attend Level 2 training, which focusses more intensively on coaching training.

---

4 See Appendix E.

Training Phase	1	2	3	4
Trainer Influence	**M** 75%	**M** 50%	**M** 25%	**M** 5%
Goal of Training	Demonstrate disciple making	Demonstrate coaching	Experience a learning community	Personal spiritual formation, ministry-specific coaching
Skills Introduced	Listening, prayer, disciple making	Reciprocal coaching, prayer, encouragement, understanding the advantages of coaching	Reciprocal teaching	Spiritual disciplines, problem solving, reciprocal coaching
Outcome for Disciples	Listening to God, training disciples using a simple system		Able to train disciples to train other disciples	Ongoing personal growth, in parallel with ongoing disciple reproduction

Figure 14: Summary of the the possible outcomes of disciple training based on the 'M' model

Our world is full of people who are looking for others who are reliable and believable. Christ-followers want to be like Jesus, so we should be the kind of people others are looking for. This is certainly a life-long learning process; we never quit learning – we always remain students in God's school.[5] The structure I described above leaves room to be sensitive to the leading and working of the Holy Spirit, and demands accountability from those who are being discipled. In the final analysis, disciples want to live out a form of discipleship that is attractive and compelling, so that the Harrys of this world (you remember…) are curious and ask: 'Is Jesus like Joe? If Jesus is like Joe, then I want to entrust my life to him.'

---

5 See Appendix C.

TEN

Empowering Leadership

Level 2: COACHES

My first vehicle was a 1956 Ford pick-up truck that I had bought for £200 when I was 15 years old. This lovely old truck, with its chrome and special design, captivated me despite the fact that I had to have it towed because it would not start. My father and I took the engine apart and discovered that the piston rods were all damaged or broken. We installed new rods and re-assembled the engine. The truck ran beautifully. No problems at all. I made sure it had enough gas, oil and water. Everything was fine, and I was happy – for six months. One day as I was driving down a busy road, I looked in my rear-view mirror and saw a thick cloud of black smoke behind me. I laughed and said to my brother, who was sitting beside me, 'The poor guy behind us has a blown engine.' I stopped at a red light and witnessed something strange: the hood of my truck began to vibrate up and down with such intensity that I thought the truck was about to take flight. An awful groaning noise came from under the hood. Suddenly we were surrounded by a thick cloud of black smoke. *I* was 'the poor guy'. It was *my* engine that was blown!

The truck was a write-off. The engine was ruined. Closer inspection showed that the oil lines were clogged and, because the oil wasn't flowing, the engine parts were destroyed by friction.

Something similar can happen to people in a church if they do not receive the attention that God intended them to get. No matter how many highly gifted volunteers a church plant has, if they don't receive sufficient care (oil), sooner or later it will lead to friction and possibly to irreparable damage. In order for training to work well and be constructive over the long term, a church needs coaching. Coaching is the lubricant that enables all of the participants in a church to keep working together smoothly, happily and without friction.

What makes a person a good coach? The answer is simple, but it is hard to put into practice: a good coach has the ability to listen well. Active listening is the most important prerequisite for good coaches.

Preparation for coaching begins with learning how to listen to others. A good active listener is able to capture the content of what a person has said and re-state it accurately in his own words. 'If I understood you correctly, you said that... Is that right?' According to Bonhoeffer, it is particularly pastors of a church who must be able to listen well. 'Christians, especially preachers, often think that they always have to have something to say when they are with other people.'[1] They forget that listening is often a greater ministry than speaking.

But even that is not enough. A good coach does not just capture the content of what is said. She also pays attention to the emotions and is able to express those in her own words: 'I'm sensing that you are feeling ... Is that right?' Men often start getting nervous at this point, because men can often be oblivious to the feelings of others. Even if they feel the other person's emotion(s), they often have trouble finding language to put into words what they are sensing. It can be helpful, therefore, for a coach to have a little cheat sheet handy. Men who have difficulty in this area may be able to find a female who can help them compose a helpful list of feeling words. Why is it so important to be able to capture a person's feelings in words? Because many people, especially women, only feel understood if someone understands their emotions.

The term 'coaching' has long been familiar to us in the world of sports. 'The term, as may be suggested by the original meaning of the word 'coach' (an enclosed carriage or rail compartment), refers to a comfortable place where a person can express her feelings, questions or concerns. The function of coaching is to prepare an athlete to perform at the highest level in situations where such performance matters.'[2]

1 Bonhoeffer, pp 83–84.
2 Schreyögg, p 7.

As we have just seen, the original context of the word 'coach' has to do with transportation and steering: a coachman holds the reins in his hands and is thereby able to steer his carriage in the desired direction. The coach itself does no work. The horses do. But the horses stay on course and reach the destination because of the work of the coachman. A coach today does the same thing: she makes it possible for others to achieve what they would not be able to do on their own. In the context of our discussion, a coach is someone who gives disciples or leaders expertise and emotional support so that they, in turn, can provide optimal care for others.

Traditional Approaches to Leader Care

The leader is left on his own (no care). This is the most common method of leading in most churches. Key leaders (staff and volunteers) have no one with whom they can talk, receive no evaluation or correction, and little encouragement. They are expected to be completely self-motivated and to learn from experience.

The leader is the recipient of teaching (care for the head). The (staff or volunteer) leader hopes to receive the tools he needs through seminars, workshops and the like in order to increase his ministry effectiveness. The disadvantage of this approach is that knowledge can be accumulated without any real learning having taken place. Real learning does not happen primarily through teaching and instruction but through putting things into practice in real-life situations, as well as through extensive conversations with those experienced in ministry and through personal reflection.

The leader receives counselling (care for the soul). (Staff and volunteer) ministry leaders may well need counselling along the way. One's own emotional health is a prerequisite for helping others to be healthy. Because counselling is focussed on the spiritual and emotional well-being of the one being counselled, questions of ministry skills and expertise are often overlooked.

The Advantages of Coaching

Prevention. Coaching is a preventative measure that can nip potential problems in the bud before they cause trouble.

Feedback. Without someone to talk with, (staff and volunteer) leaders can become tired and discouraged. When they can talk with a coach about their experiences and receive feedback, it helps – they can receive course correction and new motivation. Without honest feedback and evaluation, there is little chance of improvement and growth.

Responsibility. In a coaching relationship people are accountable. Mutually agreed upon performance standards can be evaluated, changed and improved within the context of a coaching relationship.

Multiplication. One strength of coaching is that all those involved in a ministry area can be impacted through the work of one coach with a few key leaders: the coach who meets regularly with three key leaders, for example, can thereby influence, say, thirty others. Spending concentrated time with just a few people can result in greater benefits for all.

Planning. In the 'M' model, the coach meets with a leader and with the whole group, therefore group-specific, mutually agreed upon planning can occur.

Holistic Support. A coach pays attention to skills and competencies in addition to emotional and personal issues. He provides holistic care. The goal of coaching is to walk alongside a leader or volunteer in her ministry as well as in her peronal life in such a way that successes can be celebrated, mistakes minimized, skills and gifts developed, ministry optimized, and motivation maintained.

Many disciples serving in God's kingdom lose their way or lose heart when they serve alone. An unbridled horse may produce a lot of energy and movement, but if it is undirected, energy is wasted. In many ways, Jesus dealt with his disciples like a coach. He showed them the way, kept them on track and helped them to reach certain goals. In a similar way, Christians in leadership positions (staff or volunteers) can be kept on track through the influence of a coach.

Participants in the Level 1 training were successfully trained as disciples who, in turn, have learnt to train other disciples – they proved their ability to train others. The next challenge they face is to help leaders reach their goals. As already described, it is the job of a coach to support the leaders assigned to him both in their personal growth and in the development of their ministry.

Phase 1 of disciple training in coaching

The format is the same as in Level 1 training of disciples: four units of training (weekends) spread over eight months.

- Place: A local retreat centre
- Time: Friday evening to Saturday afternoon
- Participants: 3–4 men, 3–4 women, all of whom have completed the Level 1 discipleship training, a trainer, volunteer leaders equal to the number of participant coaches
- Topic: foundations of coaching
- Goal: learn how to coach
- Materials: flip chart, markers, printed copies of the P^3O^3 Model for Coaching,[3] books for each participant (*Coaching for Commitment*, by Dennis C. Kinlaw; *Coaching for Performance*, by Sir John Whitmore)

Friday evening: After a time of worship and prayer, the trainer coaches one of the participant coaches using the P^3O^3 model, without however revealing the topics ahead of time. The remaining participants, who have been observers to this coaching session, are asked for their impressions, which are recorded on a flip chart. In groups of three, participants then discuss the benefits of coaching, and conclusions are shared with the whole group.

Saturday morning: The P^3O^3 Model for Coaching is introduced to the group. In groups of three, participant coaches practice the first three steps of the P^3O^3 model: *Personal well-being* (How are you? Tell me more); *Progress* (What have you put into practice since our last meeting?); *Praise* (for what has been put into practice). All participant coaches then gather together and describe their first coaching experience.

Lunch

Saturday afternoon: In a follow-up round, participant coachess practice the second half of the P^3O^3 model. The transition question is asked: 'What is your greatest challenge right now?' and then the model

---

3 See Fig 13 on p 146.

continues with: *Obstacles* (What obstacles will you have to overcome in order to meet this challenge?); *Options* (What possibilities do you have to meet your challenge? Which of these options seems to you to be most preferable?); *Outcomes* (What practical steps will you take to help you meet your challenge before our next meeting in eight weeks?) The goals set should be SMART (*S*pecific, *M*easurable, *A*ttainable, *R*elevant, *T*ime-limited, i.e., having a deadline).

The trainer rounds out the weekend with a short talk on the benefits of coaching. A number of volunteer leaders from the church equal to the number of participant coaches joins the group at the end of the afternoon.

Conclude with coffee break and conversation

Homework: Participant coaches are paired with the volunteer leaders from the church and agree on two dates within the next eight weeks when they will meet for coaching. The two books mentioned earlier (by Kinlaw and by Whitmore) are given to each participant coach and are to be read by the next training weekend.

Two months pass.

Phase 2 of disciple training in coaching

- Place: a local retreat centre
- Time: Friday to Saturday afternoon
- Participants: 3–4 men, 3–4 women, a trainer
- Topic: foundations of coaching
- Goal: learn how to coach
- Materials: flip chart, markers

Friday evening: After a time of worship and prayer, participant coaches report on their first two coaching sessions with the volunteer leaders assigned to them. The trainer introduces GROW as an aid for coaching. The four letters of GROW stand for steps in healthy growth: *G*oal-setting asks the questions: 'What do you want to accomplish? What do you want to see changed?' *R*eality asks the questions: 'What have you done thus far to reach your goals? What were the results?' *O*ptions asks the questions: 'What are your options? What would happen if….' *W*hat will you do? asks the questions: 'What will you do to meet your goals before our next meeting? When? Will you really meet your goals with these steps?' The participant coaches gather in groups of three and each participant identifies a problem they have encountered in their coaching experience. These problems are discussed using GROW questions and possible solutions are proposed. Results are reported to the entire group.

Saturday morning: In groups of three, participant coaches name helpful insights they have gleaned from the two coaching books they have read. Afterwards these insights are shared with the entire group.

Lunch

Saturday afternoon: The trainer gives a short talk on the power of open questions (as opposed to closed questions). Open questions are ones that cannot be answered with 'yes' or 'no'. The power of open questions is that they stimulate thought and reflection. They enable penetration into the deeper levels of a problem, topic or situation. In groups of three, participant coaches suggest open questions for the coaching process. These are then reported to the whole group.

Conclude with coffee break and conversation

Homework: Participant coaches continue their coaching sessions with their partnered leaders from the church. In addition, they each invite their partner leader to the next training day.

Two months pass.

Phase 3 of disciple training in coaching

- Place: a local retreat centre
- Time: Saturday
- Participants: 3–4 men, 3–4 women, a trainer, the volunteer leaders from the church who are in a coaching relationship with one of the participants
- Topic: helping leaders become coaches
- Goal: to teach the leaders, who up till now have been coached by the participants, to be coaches themselves
- Materials: flip chart, markers, P^3O^3 model[4]

Saturday morning: After a time of worship and prayer, the trainer asks the volunteer leaders present to report how they have benefited from the coaching sessions they have experienced. Results are captured on a flip chart.

The participant coaches agree among themselves who will describe which step of the P^3O^3 model. After 15 minutes of preparation, the participant coaches explain the steps of the model to the volunteer leaders. Afterwards each of the volunteer leaders receives a handout of the P^3O^3 model. They are then asked to practice the first three steps of the model with their participant coaches (i.e., the roles are now reversed: the volunteer leaders, who have been coached before, assume the coaching role).

Lunch

Saturday afternoon: The volunteer leaders report the first impressions of their experience as coaches to the entire group. Then they work through the last half of the model in groups of three as before. A discussion of the benefits of coaching rounds out the day.

Conclude with coffee break and conversation

Homework: The participants continue to meet with and coach the volunteer leaders. In addition, each of these leaders is asked to identify someone in their ministry area with whom they will

---

4 See Fig 13 on p 146.

conduct two coaching sessions based on the P^3O^3 model over the next two months.

Two months pass.

Phase 4 of disciple training in coaching

- Place: a local retreat centre
- Time: Saturday morning
- Participants: 3–4 men, 3–4 women, a trainer, the volunteer leaders from the church who are in a coaching relationship with one of the participants
- Topic: sharpen the coaching skills of the volunteer leaders
- Goal: to complete the coaching process and introduce the next level of training
- Materials: flip chart, markers

Saturday morning: After a time of worship and prayer, the group is divided into participant coaches and volunteer leaders (those who have been coached). The coaches are asked to discuss the following questions: What have I learned as a coach thus far? Where do I have room for improvement (my growth edge)? The leaders are asked to consider how their own ministry with others could be improved through coaching and what they need to see this happen. This level of training ends with a *Lectio Divina* exercise.

Conclude with lunch and conversation

Level 3: MINISTRY-AREA LEADERS

Leading an entire ministry area is quite different from leading as a coach or a disciple who takes initiative. Therefore there is a separate level of training for ministry leaders. Ministry leaders carry a lot of responsibility, but because of their position, experience and competence it is often assumed that they do not need training – they surely know what it means to be a 'healthy' leader, who leads a 'healthy' team, which in turn does its part to carry out 'healthy' ministry in the church.

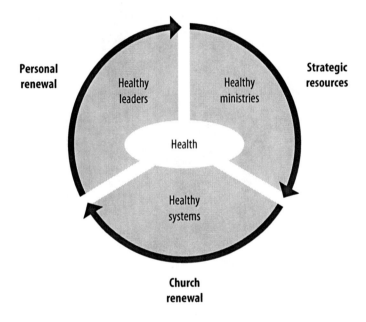

Figure 15: A paradigm of spiritual health[5]

In order to safeguard the spiritual health of a church, pay attention to the spiritual health of three areas of church life: ministries, systems and leaders. The spiritual health of the leaders has the highest priority of the three, because it enables the other two. The leaders' personal renewal always precedes renewal within a church. For this reason one must invest in the

---

5 After Terry Walling, from a lecture at Fuller Theological Seminary, Pasadena, CA, on 15 June 2001: "Essentials of Corporate Revitalization: Refocusing Your Ministry."

training of healthy leaders. It is essential in planting healthy churches. The training of ministry leaders is designed to meet this need.

The training occurs in the same format as the other two levels of training we have described already – that of disciples and coaches – and takes eight months. The participants are chosen by the trainer or facilitator from the pool of those who have completed disciple training in mentoring and coaching, and who are already exercising leadership in a ministry area, such as children's work, missions, pastoral care, small groups, admin, hospitality, etc.

Phase 1 of training ministry-area leaders

Prior to the training, participants are asked to read the following five books:

John C. Maxwell: *Developing the Leader Within You*

Patrick Lencioni: *The Five Dysfunctions of a Team*

Robert Logan and Carl George: *Leading and Managing Your Church*

Sandy Kulkin: *The DISC Personality System – Enhance Communication and Relationships*

Dietrich Schindler: *The Jesus Model*

- Place: a local retreat centre
- Time: Friday to Saturday afternoon
- Participants: 3–4 men, 3–4 women, all of whom have completed the training as disciples and as coaches, a trainer
- Topic: personality characteristics and spiritual leadership
- Goal: participants learn to recognize and understand their own personality profile and learn the foundational principles of spiritual leadership from the life of Jesus
- Materials: flip chart, markers, the books mentioned above, the Gospel of Matthew

Friday evening: After introductions, worship and prayer, a trainer talks briefly about the three essential areas of health (self, ministry, leadership) before introducing the DISC profile. Participants are asked to identify their own personality profile using the questions listed in the book for this purpose. Results are reported to the group. Then the trainer talks shortly about the various personality types and their interaction with one another.

Saturday morning: The group gathers together and the trainer reminds everyone that leadership has to do with influence. Jesus influenced people to love God and one another and to fulfil God's plan for their lives. Participants form groups of two, and using the Gospel of Matthew, which is divided into four sections, discover ways Jesus influenced others. Conclusions are discussed with the entire group. To provide further understanding, participants discuss differences between Jesus' leadership and secular leadership.

Lunch

Saturday afternoon: Participants form groups of three. They discuss the learning from the morning session, how it impinges upon what they experienced when they coached volunteer leaders during their coach training, and what they might have done differently. Results are shared with the whole group.

Homework: Reflect on the content of the books, noting their most important points. The participant leaders meet with the other leaders in their ministry area to articulate their vision for their ministry area and answer three questions: What's our next step? Why is this our next step? What resources are available to us for this step?

Conclude with coffee break and conversation.

Two months pass.

Phase 2 of training ministry-area leaders

- Place: A local retreat centre
- Time: Friday to Saturday afternoon
- Participants: 3–4 men, 3–4 women, a trainer
- Topic: moving from vision to concrete results
- Goal: ministry leaders learn to work with the leaders in their ministry area in a goal-oriented way
- Materials: flip chart, markers, the books mentioned above

Friday evening: After a time of worship and prayer, participant leaders share the results of their homework, which was to meet with the other leaders in their ministry area to develop vision statements and plan next steps. In groups of three they are asked to now further develop their plans using the waterfall diagram in the book by Logan and George. Results are shared with the whole group.

Saturday morning: The trainer gives a short talk about the five elements of a successful team according to Lencioni. Then in groups of three, participants discuss how to apply these five elements in their own areas of ministry. The following questions should guide the discussion: Which of these five elements are strong or weak in my ministry area. Why? What can I do as ministry leader to eliminate weakness? What SMART goals will I pursue in the next two months?

Lunch

Saturday afternoon: Each participant takes 30 minutes to reflect on the most important leadership principle in Maxwell's book. How will the participants implement this principle in their ministries? Share and pray for this in the whole group. Lastly, the group discusses where the principles in Maxwell's book are seen in the life of Jesus and how Jesus embodied them.

Conclude with coffee break and conversation

Homework: Begin implementing the plans that have been worked on, and report on this next time.

Two months pass.

Phase 3 of training ministry-area leaders

- Place: a local retreat centre
- Time: Saturday
- Participants: 3–4 men, 3–4 women, a trainer, volunteer leaders from the ministry areas
- Topic: ensuring leaders get coaching
- Goal: ministry leaders coach the volunteer leaders under their care
- Materials: flip chart, markers

Saturday morning: After a time of worship and prayer, participant leaders report what they have implemented since the last training session. Successes are celebrated. Obstacles are discussed and solutions proposed to overcome them. The trainer coaches one of the participant leaders in an area of his ministry where he would like to see change, while the other participant leaders observe. Because all participant leaders have already received training as coaches, they are able to discuss in groups of three the use of coaching with the people under their care. They do this using the SWOT analysis: *S*trengths, *W*eaknesses, *O*pportunities, *T*hreats. Results are reported to the whole group.

Lunch

Saturday afternoon: Volunteer leaders from the ministry areas of the participant leaders join the session after lunch. The participant leaders work with them on answering two specific questions: How can our ministry area work in ways that are more goal oriented? What can we do to raise up more leaders? Results are discussed in the whole group. This training is ended with a time of prayer.

Conclude with coffee break and conversation

Homework: Participant leaders start coaching the volunteer leaders under their care.

Two months pass.

Phase 4 of training ministry-area leaders

- Place: a local retreat centre
- Time: Saturday
- Participants: 3–4 men, 3–4 women, a trainer
- Topic: accountability and needs
- Goal: to uncover and address previously unrecognized needs of the ministry leaders
- Materials: flip chart, markers

Saturday morning: After a time of worship and prayer, participant leaders report on their work of implementing a goal-oriented approach, as well as on the coaching they have done with the leaders under their care. Successes are celebrated. The trainer asks the participant leaders to discuss the following question in groups of three: 'What do you as a ministry-area leader need in order for your work and that of your leaders and volunteers to be more effective?' Responses are discussed in the whole group. Suggested solutions are discussed and captured on a flip chart. A time of prayer ends the session.

Lunch

Homework: Ministry-area leaders are invited to take part in the training for church planters.

Level 4: CHURCH PLANTERS

One sign of a healthy church is that it can reproduce, and it does so. The New Testament bears this out. The churches in Syria and Antioch had their origins in Jerusalem. The Holy Spirit sent Paul and Barnabas from Antioch to plant churches in Asia Minor. In his seminal work about the missionary activities of the early church, Roland Allen argues convincingly that Paul planted churches that, in turn, multiplied within their respective geographic regions. In no more than ten years, Paul established churches in four provinces of the Roman Empire: Galatia, Macedonia, Achaia and Asia. Before AD 47 there were no churches in these provinces. By AD 57 Paul was able to say that his work was done. He could take extended trips far to the west without any fear that the churches he had planted would die due to lack of leadership and support.[6]

Healthy churches reproduce themselves both regionally and beyond the borders of their own culture. In order for this to happen, the appropriate vision as well as a methodology to train church planters must be in place. Church planters will have to come increasingly from the ranks of those who have had no formal theological education. They will have to come from churches that provide fertile soil and have a conducive atmosphere for the training of church-planting teams. The 'M' model will again serve as a basis for the training.

---

6 Allen, *Missionary Methods*, p 3.

Phase 1 of disciple training in church planting

Those who are invited to this final level of leadership training have proven themselves as mentors to other Christ-followers. Ideally the group will consist of five to eight participants. The goal of this training is to put a team of active, committed disciples in the position to start a new church and guide its healthy development.

- Place: a local retreat centre
- Time: Friday to Saturday afternoon
- Participants: 3–4 men, 3–4 women, all of whom have completed the training as ministry leaders, a trainer or facilitator
- Topic: building bridges to non-Christians
- Goal: to understand the importance of relationally-oriented ministry and learn how to practice this
- Materials: flip chart, markers, book (*The Jesus Model*), the Gospel of Matthew

Friday evening: After introductions, worship and prayer, the facilitator gives a short talk on the topic 'Jesus and his Relationship to Lost People,' based on Matthew 9:35–38. The trainer or facilitator then reminds the participant church planters of the concept of a relational network, discussed in the book *The Jesus Model.* In groups of three, participants answer the question: 'If you want to spend half of your time building a network of relationships with non-Christians, what would that look like, practically speaking?' Results are discussed in the larger group.

Saturday morning: The trainer gives a talk based on the book *The Jesus Model* and briefly outlines the steps of this model. In groups of three, participants discuss these questions: 'Which of these steps presents the greatest challenge for me?' 'What support will I need in order to be able to plant a church according to this model?' 'How can I deepen my relationship to my Father in heaven?' Results are discussed in the larger group and captured on a flip chart.

Lunch

Saturday afternoon: Participants divide into two groups, called 'pods' (a term used for a small school of marine animals – an individual's learning can be expanded if the learning process is experienced together with others). Each pod views itself as a church-planting team that will plan and execute the planting of a new church. The pods arrive at an answer to the question: 'How can we, individually and together, live intentionally and continuously in the presence of God our Father?' Responses are shared with the whole group.

The day concludes with a *Lectio Divina* exercise.

Coffee break and conversation

Homework: The pods meet every other week, work through *The Jesus Model* and write down three to five achievable steps for each section, which they want to put into practice as a church-planting team. The goal is to work through the book *The Jesus Model* in four meetings. At the next training session, the pod will detail the three to five concrete steps from each section that they intend to put into practice.

Two months pass.

Phase 2 of disciple training in church planting

- Place: a local retreat centre
- Time: Friday to Saturday afternoon
- Participants: 3–4 men, 3–4 women, a trainer
- Topic: the nature and function of a church and the four phases of church planting
- Goal: to understand the nature and function of a church as well as the four phases of church planting, and to develop a plan to put this into practice
- Materials: flip chart, markers, book (*The Jesus Model*)

Friday evening: After worship and prayer, the trainer asks the participant church planters to report what they have to celebrate from their homework assignment. One representative from each pod reports his group's results, which are captured on a flip chart. A handout is distributed containing an outline of *The Jesus Model*[7] and including suggestions for implementing each step. Participants have sufficient time to discuss both the work of the pods as well as the prepared handout.

Saturday morning: The trainer gives a short talk about the nature of the church according to the New Testament. Then the trainer or another facilitator gives a short talk about the function of a church (evangelism – worship – community – discipleship). The pods discuss the content of these talks: 'How is this understanding of the nature and function of a church similar to or different from what we have experienced personally in the churches we have known?' 'How will our church plant be different from church as we've experienced it to date?' Results are shared in the large group.

Lunch

Saturday afternoon: The trainer gives a brief talk about the four-phase 'M' model. There is time for questions. Then each pod is asked to choose a city or a neighbourhood where they want to plant a church. Afterwards the pod considers the question: 'What might this church

---

7 See Fig 1 on p 19.

look like in five years, if God blesses our plans?' Responses are shared in the large group, followed by a time of prayer.

Homework: The pods continue to meet every other week and work on three assignments: i) the vision for the new church; ii) demographic information about the target area; iii) each team member starts to build a network of relationships among non-Christians in their targeted area.

Two months pass.

Phase 3 of disciple training in church planting

- Place: a local retreat centre
- Time: Saturday
- Participants: 3–4 men, 3–4 women, a trainer, two external church-planting coaches, who will be coaching the church planter and his team
- Topic: mutual inspiration and overcoming obstacles
- Goal: mutual inspiration and identifying measures to be taken to overcome obstacles
- Materials: flip chart, markers, book (*The Jesus Model*)

Saturday morning: After worship and prayer, representatives of the pods share the results of their work during the past two months: vision statements, insights from demographic data, relational networks. Time is given for interaction. Each pod discusses the question: 'What are the greatest obstacles we face to the successful establishment of a healthy church?' Responses are discussed in the large group and captured on a flip chart.

Saturday afternoon: A church-planting coach is assigned to each pod. The coach discusses the obstacles and possible solutions. SMART goals are established. In the large group each pod then shares the obstacles and solutions they have discussed. The pods pray for each other.

Conclude with coffee break and discussion

Homework: Continue meeting every other week. The church-planting coach should also attend these meetings. Each coach tracks progress and records[8] what measures their assigned pod has decided to take, based on *The Jesus Model*. Now for the first time, new people – Christians and non-Christians – are invited to participate in the church-planting project.

---

8 Use the checklists in Appendix A.

Phase 4 of disciple training in church planting

- Place: A local retreat centre
- Time: Saturday
- Participants: 3–4 men, 3–4 women, facilitators, two church-planting coaches
- Topic: preview services and the integration of new people
- Goal: planning 2–3 preview worship services and developing a plan for assimilating new people
- Materials: flip chart, markers, book (*The Jesus Model*)

Saturday morning: After worship and prayer, representatives of each pod share the results of their homework assignments: the revised catalogue of measures to be taken ('What has changed since the initial planning?'), expansion of the start-up team, and successes are celebrated through prayers of thanksgiving. The pods are asked to create a flow chart for the assimilation of new people, from their first visit to their involvement as a ministry leader. It should be clearly visible on one sheet of paper how people are trained as disciples, become active volunteers, apprentice leaders and leaders. The same diagram should portray the interconnection of the various ministries in the church. Results are shared with the large group.

Lunch

Saturday afternoon: The coach of each pod explains the strengths and weaknesses of the church-planting initiative using a SWOT analysis. SMART goals are established to eliminate the weaknesses. The coach helps the pod develop a plan for the first two to three preview worship services. Results are shared with the large group. In a final round each pod asks the question: 'When will this new (not yet planted) church plant its first daughter church?' Using the waterfall diagram (Logan/George, *Leading and Managing Your Church*), the rough draft of an initial plan is developed. A member of the pod is given the job of overseeing the process of the next church plant. These results are shared with the large group as well. The training ends with a time of worship to the glory of God.

Conclude with coffee break and conversation

Homework: The church-planting coaches continue to guide the new church plants until the first daughter church is established.

Values Underpinning the 'M' Model

In the final analysis, our values drive our behaviour. One can articulate values without practicing them. Nevertheless our values are close to our hearts. What are the assumptions that underpin the 'M' model and ensure its success? They are values that have to do with the learning process.

This model assumes that 'to learn' means 'to do'. Our contemporary Western system of learning is derived from Greek and Roman thinking. Ancient Greek education was knowledge based: a person had learned when a concept had been understood, answers had been given and a programme of study had been completed. The ancient Hebrew concept was markedly different: not until a person had put into practice the things he learned was that person considered a successful learner. The wise and the righteous, as described in the wisdom literature of the Old Testament, were those who led a life actively dedicated to God. But a large part of contemporary Christian education and training is knowledge-based. The 'M' model, by contrast, demands active involvement from the participants – exactly what produces real learning. Jesus commanded us to be 'teaching them to obey everything I have commanded you' (Matthew 28:20), i.e., to put it into practice. Active obedience is the proof of successful learning.

To learn means to make progress without being overwhelmed by all that remains to be learned: 'Do the first thing first, one thing at a time, just one more task.'[9]

To learn also means to learn together, in community with others. Some teams are not much more than groups of individuals thrown together, each person doing her part without much vision for the whole. Accomplishing a task together is as important as learning together. No one person has all the answers. No one person is always strong. No one person is always highly motivated and engaged. By learning together, teams experience the spiritual power of the many 'one another' passages that occur in the writings of the Apostle Paul. This is the core of what Bonhoeffer described in his classic work *Life Together*.

Learning means relationships as well. This is clear from the previous paragraph, but more than that: the fruit of the Spirit (Galatians 5:22–23)

---

9 One of Neil Cole's pithy maxims.

grows out of healthy relationships. Only within the context of relationships can I learn to forgive, to love, to be patient, to carry another's burden, not to be covetous and so on. Spiritual growth – life change – happens in the context of relationships. When God speaks clearly to his children, they live out his words among his children – relationships are God's classroom.

Finally, to learn means to reproduce. Gifting and intuition are not transferable. A person who has vast amounts of experience in Christian leadership is not often able to communicate that experience to others. But the 'M' model is a systematic process that can yield more and better leaders, because learning always flows towards another person to influence him towards Jesus.

Tips for Coaching Church Planters

Effective coaching of church planters and their teams often makes the difference between success and failure in the venture. The coaching structure described can be helpful in order to ensure that coaches keep the end in mind during every phase of the new church's development and are wise consultants to the church planters.

Before the first steps in church planting are taken, there is much to consider. A coach can help a church planter to organize her thoughts. A coach can also help to ensure that no signficant area of planning is overlooked. The following are topics that a coach will keep in mind when helping to guide the church-planting team through the decisive phases of the church's development.

God's vision in the heart of the church planter
The thought gives birth to the deed. A church comes into being in the same way every creation does – twice: before being born, it is first born in the heart and mind of the creator. The *idea* to plant a church contains four elements:

- God's vision for the world: evangelism (missional, incarnational)
- God's vision for his people: church (worship, new community that represents God's kingdom)

- God's vision for a specific geographic community: lost people (mercy and justice, cultural relevance)
- God's vision for the timing: *kairos* / open doors

The idea to plant a church

Approximately two to six months before the church-planting project is started, the following issues must be deliberated and then checked off the list when they have been resolved:

_____Prayerful reflection upon the most important Bible passages concerning mission and evangelism

_____Regular (daily) prayer to determine whether God wants this church to be planted

_____Reading of literature (books, articles) about church planting

_____Clarity about motives and God's leading

_____Affirmation and blessing from the mother church (sending church) for the church-planting venture

_____A person identified and engaged to coach the church planter and the church-planting team

_____A decision taken by the church planter and church-planting team to participate in a network of church planters

All points considered on_____

Remember

After each phase, the church planter does three things with his team:

- Evaluation – What went well? What has to be improved?
- Consultation – What does the coach think about the developments?
- Celebration – All glory to God, and thanks and recognition to the team and all volunteers.

When Christ Jesus calls people to the important ministry of church planting, it is essential that, guided by the Holy Spirit, they find a doable way of successfully accomplishing the mission. I am convinced that this book contains the necessary tools needed by those entrusted with the leadership of a church-planting endeavour to take one step at a time and not be overwhelmed. Nothing is more frustrating than knowing a job needs to be done but not knowing how to do it.

ELEVEN

Intentional Multiplication

One significant difference between Jesus and his disciples can often be found in Jesus' vision: he always saw further and wider than his followers did. When we start to see through Jesus' eyes when it comes to church planting, we will stop looking at what *is* and start noticing what *could be*. To make a good start, we need a good end in sight – something that God has in mind.

Jesus saw *multiplication*. He compared the workers in his kingdom with a farmer. A farmer is not someone who thinks 1:1, but rather 1:60 or 1:100 (cf. Mark 4). The early church took Jesus' perspective to heart and put it into practice. There was a new church *every day* in the time of the Apostles: 'So the churches were strengthened in faith and grew daily in numbers' (Acts 16:5).

Paul planted churches that quickly became self-sufficient and reproductive. He assumed that the believers would become missionaries (1 Thessalonians 1:8), that churches would plant other churches, and that whole regions would be evangelized, which is why Paul could write in Romans 15:18–19: 'For I will not venture to speak of anything except what Christ has accomplished through me to win obedience from the Gentiles, by word and deed, by the power of signs and wonders, by the power of the Holy Spirit of God, so *that from Jerusalem and as far around as Illyricum I have fully proclaimed the good news of Christ*' (NRSV, Anglicized, author's emphasis).

Planting a church is good. Planting a church that in turn plants another church is even better. To move from addition to multiplication, we must think differently. From the very first step, we have to move differently, plan differently and work differently. Not only Jesus' teaching and the example of the early church compel us in this direction. The world in which we live also makes multiplication a necessity.

If we are realistic, the development of the spiritual landscape in Europe gives us cause for concern. In England in 1991, George Carey, the former Anglican Archbishop, compared his church to an elderly lady 'who mutters away to herself in a corner, ignored most of the time.'[1] Since then hundreds of churches have closed their doors each year while at the same time many new Islamic worship centres have been opening their doors. London, with approximately 300 mosques and 500 madrassas (Koran schools), can lay claim to the title of Islamic capital of Europe. During the Olympic games in 2012, visitors could hardly miss seeing the largest mosque in the Western world, located just 400 metres from the Olympic Village. Already in 2004 it was reported that regular attendance at mosques in Britain exceeded the number of regular worshippers attending Church of England services.[2]

Apparently the number of those within the European Union who consider themselves Muslim grows by a million each year. In France the growth of Islam is greater than anywhere else in Europe. Ten per cent of the French population is now Muslim. More mosques and madrassas have been built in France in the last thirty years than Catholic churches have been built in the last 100 years.[3] The rapid decline of Christianity coupled with the growth of Islam prompted dire predictions that the rise of Islam will unleash a cultural crisis in Europe.[4]

Not only in England and France, but also in Germany the influence of Christianity is fast waning. In the last decade, the Protestant church in Germany has closed 10 per cent of its church buildings due to financial reasons.[5] Sunday church attendance in Germany's major cities is less than 2 per cent. Philip Jenkins writes that while in 1900 two thirds of the world's

---

1 George Carey, in 1991, in an interview by Russell Twisk for *Reader's Digest* on Carey's appointment as the next Archbishop of Canterbury. Seen in February 2013 at: http://www.thetablet.co.uk/article/3958
2 As sourced in February 2013 from: http://timesofindia.indiatimes.com/articleshow/444572.cms See also: http://www.gatestoneinstitute.org/2761/converting-churches-into-mosques
3 Sourced in February 2013 at: http://www.catholicnewsagency.com/new.php?n=7990
4 Huntington, pp 217–18.
5 This statistic was communicated to the author in an e-mail from the Office of Statistics of the Evangelical Church of Germany on 17 January 2005.

Christians were found in Europe, it is now less than one fourth, and by the year 2025 it is estimated to be less than one fifth.[6] The news magazine *Der Spiegel* accurately expressed the weakening of German Christianity when it reported that, 'Germany is a pagan land with remnants of Christianity.'[7]

Alongside the better-known large state churches (Lutheran, Reformed, United), the Free Churches also merit mention. About 1 per cent of Germany's population belongs to a Free Church (smaller denominations and independent churches).[8] It is these Free Churches that have experienced growth in the last forty years through the planting of new congregations. In ten years the Free Churches in Germany have planted 1500 new churches, while in the same time period 200 churches have closed their doors.[9] However, most people who start attending a newly planted Free Church are Christians from other congregations. It is beyond question that the Free Churches have made progress, but there are still far too few of these congregations. The population at large hardly notices them and they are not changing the culture. Programmes intended to produce growth have had only limited success. If we liken the large state churches to supermarkets, then the Free Churches are like delis – great for gourmet food, but not in a position to satisfy the hunger of the masses.

Even the planting of individual new churches is hardly going to reverse the downward trend of de-Christianization that is taking place in Germany and in the rest of Europe. For example, experts predict an 18 per cent population decline in Germany, from 82 million in 2009 to a possible 67 million in 2050, despite the addition of 100,000 new immigrants each year. Over the same period, the Protestant and Catholic churches are projected to shrink by about 25 per cent. Germany's population will become both numerically smaller and in terms of religion, less Christian. How can this trend be reversed in Germany and elsewhere in Europe? Church planting is a good start but is not enough. A new approach is

---

6 Jenkins, pp 2–3.
7 Werner Harenberg, "Spiegel-Umfrage über Glauben und Religion, Kirchen und Kirchensteuer" [English translation: Survey of faith, religion, church, and church tax], *Der Spiegel* #25, 15 June 1992, p 36.
8 In 2003 the member churches of the Federation of Free Churches had a total of 859,000 members. In comparison to Germany's population of 82.5 million, this is approximately 1% of the country's population.
9 Karsten Huhn, "Gründerzeiten", *Idea Spektrum* #25, 2004, p 16.

needed, which will enable healthy, rapid church growth with the power to effect social transformation. This can only happen through a 'church-planting multiplication movement' that has shifted from the addition of new churches to the multiplication of new churches.

In my experience of over twenty years as a church planter in Germany, I have come to identify six qualities that set apart great church planting from merely good church planting. I refer to them as the 'G7': timed release, generational distance, discipleship depth, intentional mindset, external focus, a multiplication coordinator, and reproducible models.

The 'G7' Qualities of Great Church Planting

Church Planting by 'Addition'	vs	Church Planting by 'Multiplication'
Long recovery time		Timed release
Direct involvement		Generational distance
Emphasis on leadership		Discipleship depth
Haphazard and situational		Intentional mindset
Centripetal force		External focus
Near-sightedness		Multiplication coordinator
Emphasis on giftedness		Reproducible models

Figure 16: Two ways of planting churches

Timed release

To treat the symptoms of the flu, colds, headaches and insomnia, pharmaceutical companies have given us the ubiquitous tiny time-release capsules. They are tiny controlled-release systems engineered to provide on-going medication, sometimes with one kind of treatment beginning to work when another has exhausted its capacity. Church planting by multiplication incorporates the concept of timed release. Timed release is the discipline of setting the date of the next church plant shortly after the current church has been launched.

Too often I have observed a mother church, after having planted a daughter, going into what seemed like an unusually long recovery period. In our European context it might take a decade or more before a church summons enough resolve and resources to begin another daughter church. It is the fate of new churches that fail to begin with the end in mind, i.e., the planting of a new church.

Church-planting churches will hardly highly impact their society with the power of the gospel in increments of ten or twenty years. The discipline of timed release keeps before us the goal of launching new churches in shorter periods of time – after one to three, or at the maximum, five years. Every five years high-impact churches will see to it that a new church is birthed from their midst. To use another analogy, every five years these churches set a timer to run down to the date of their next launch and do all in their power, trusting God, to see a new 'life' set free.

Generational distance

Whereas timed release is the discipline of chain-reaction church planting, generational distance is where multiplication begins to set in. My wife's grandparents were married for more than seventy-five years when they died. Grandpa was 105 and Grandma 97 years old, and they left behind over 150 progeny. In their lifetime they saw themselves forwarded into five generations! Imagine holding a fifth-generation baby in your arms, knowing you and your spouse were the first cause! How effective a mother church is in forwarding itself via ensuing church plants reflects the issue of generational distance. Thus multiplying churches focus not so much on the churches they have spawned, but on the number of generations that they have spawned. Church planting by multiplication counts the generations, not just the number of children it has fostered.

This is the heart of multiplication: for multiplication to occur, the first cause of new life must free itself from direct involvement. Even the best grandparents do not give birth directly to their grandchildren but indirectly. Direct involvement is the vocabulary of addition: one church starting another church via direct influence. Multiplication is effective because of its indirection: one church setting its offspring free to procreate churches. Generational distance is an emphasis that has rarely occurred in our European setting, but it is a key ingredient needed for multiplication to take place.

Discipleship depth

Why is it that the vast majority of churches never experience such a level of church-planting growth? The answer lies in the third dimension: discipleship depth. This takes seriously Jesus' command that his followers produce other life-long learners of Jesus. Dallas Willard paraphrases our clarion call beautifully: *'I have been given say over everything on heaven and earth. So go make apprentices to me among people of every kind. Submerge them in the reality of the Trinitarian God. And lead them into doing everything I have told you to do. Now look! I am with you every minute, until the job is completely done!'* (Matthew 28:18–20).[10]

The quality of depth in multiplying churches is directly linked to how well disciples are made who, in turn, make disciples. The constant need for new leadership is the challenge of church multiplication. But good leadership begins with good discipleship. A proven disciple is the best foundation for an influential leader. In short, making disciples that make disciples becomes the launching pad for churches planting churches.

To get to the place where discipleship is intentional, reproducing, evangelistic, and leading to leadership development, we need more than gifted leaders. We will value and implement healthy systems of discipleship training that are better than the people using them. A healthy system of reproduction does good things to all involved. It instills Christ-likeness into people in a manner in which they cannot do it alone.

Multiplying churches witness life change and healthy growth in their smallest life units: small groups or triads. Churches reproduce rapidly externally because they have been systematically reproducing internally: the disciple-making members will live with timed-release dates. It is assumed in such churches that non-Christians as well as believers will make strides in coming to Christ or maturing in Christ.

As an example: Parallel to our small-group Bible studies, we fostered triad discipleship groups in our fellowship in Kaiserslautern. One year a man in his early thirties by the name of Falk gave his life to Jesus. I promptly invited him to join two others along with myself in a mini-group. The group divided and Falk and I began our next group with a young man who

---

10 Willard, *Renovation of the Heart*, pp 240–42; *The Great Omission*, p xiii.

was seeking. The three of us read three chapters in the Bible daily and met together weekly to share and pray with one another. Our weekly check-ups regularly dealt with topics pertaining to family, temptation, finances, anger, and sharing our faith. I saw so much change in Falk's life as a result of high biblical intake and regular sharing of how we were doing in our daily walk with Christ.

Intentional mindset

The will to want church growth is the engine that drives it.[11] The same applies to church planting by multiplication vs addition. It must be intentionally pursued for it to occur. No person has ever drifted into becoming a concert pianist; in the same way, a church-planting movement will never happen by chance.

Inspiring vision and deeply felt need are the fuel that propel purposeful action. God inspired the patriarchs by transmitting wide-eyed pictures to them of what was to come: teeming masses of people as countless as the stars of the heavens or the sand granules on the seashore. A truly inspiring vision sees the future with the grandeur of God and draws the onlooker into it as surely as metal is attracted to a magnet.

But even the most compelling vision loses its drawing power with time. The builders of the wall around Jerusalem were obviously inspired by Nehemiah's vision. They set to work immediately. Yet this vision did not stop them from interrupting what they were doing. In their case, the vision lost its lustre after 26 days, and they subsequently left off doing the work. Vision is like a campfire: it cools off with time and thus needs periodic stoking, preferably monthly, for people to remain committed to it.

Vision by itself, even if periodically 'stoked', is insufficient to propel most people toward action. Inspiration needs the additive of deeply felt need. Need propels us to act. Spiritual and social movers and shakers such as Martin Luther King Jr., William Wilberforce, Madame Curie or Mother Theresa bear this out.

My father died at the age of 58. His death was brought on by a heart attack that was preceded by kidney failure. Knowing this, my doctor urged me to have my kidneys checked annually. I nodded in assent – and did

---

11 Wagner, p 39.

nothing. That is until one morning when I noticed symptoms that could be indicators of kidney problems. Within an hour and a half I was sitting in the office of a specialist. What brought about the change in behaviour was not the vision; it was my deeply felt personal need. To see blood where I did not expect it spurred me into action. (Thankfully the problem is gone.)

A great church-planting multiplication movement shifts into gear by feeling the brokenness, hurt and pain of those not being reached by conventional churches. Jesus was angered and smitten by the hardness of heart of some of his hearers (Mark 2:5); he was in psychosomatic pain over the lostness of the lost (Matthew 9:36). It was this deeply felt sorrow over that state of the heart of the lost that propelled him and his followers to move into the harvest.

It has been thirty years, but I still remember the first sentence spoken by my first homiletics professor in my first hour in his class. Quietly yet firmly Dr. Holmes said, 'Most of you will not become great preachers (pause), because you do not *plan* on becoming great preachers.' Intentionality is the mother of quality. Though not guaranteeing a qualitative spiritual movement, such a movement is not the by-product of chance, but of intentionality.

Early on in the church plant in Kaiserslautern I secured a colourful bag of plastic locomotives from a toy store. As people became members of the church, each was given a locomotive to place on her desk at home. The locomotive was a visual 'pun'. We told our people that we were praying and working towards establishing new 'train stations', namely new churches (our church in Kaiserslautern at that time met in the building of a former railway refectory). We put church planting in our literature, talked of it often, did it, and are intent on continuing to do it. This is intentionality at work.

External focus

Our values determine where we spend our time. Thus our behaviour will always serve to bring our true beliefs to the surface. Behaviour is belief in action. We may profess the importance of seeking the lost, but where we spend our time proves what we truly consider important. The men and women behind great church-planting ministries spend lots of time with those they are called to reach. As they do this, they behave as Jesus did. He was *internally* motivated while being *externally* oriented.

Many people in ministry spend time with the already reached; this is where they devote their energies. The study desk can become a convenient barrier to time spent with the lost. We must overcome this barrier. When we look at where Jesus spent his weekdays, we see him in the harvest, criss-crossing Galilee with half-baked, not yet truly convinced but truly seeking, followers.

The older a ministry grows, the stronger is the gravitational pull towards the insiders. Gravity is the problem to overcome if we want to get from Frankfurt to Chicago. To get from the barn to the harvest, we need to be externally oriented and pull ourselves away from the inward pull of the church.

In the first two years of our church plant in Kaiserslautern I intentionally visited over 400 businesses personally. I purposefully asked to speak with each boss, stating that I was the new pastor of a new church in town and as such wanted to meet our 'neighbours'. Some significant and memorable conversations, some ending in prayer, resulted from those visits. I certainly had enough to do without seeking out the business community, but I realized that I needed regular contact with non-Christians – and they needed a Christian in their life.

If we really want to see a church-planting multiplication movement occur, we will emphasize the size of each individual's *OIKOS*.[12] Each person's *OIKOS* is his relational network. To discover our evangelistic *OIKOS* we will note the names of every person with whom we spend an hour or more in an average week who is not a follower of Jesus. These are people with whom we are naturally relating: we have natural inroads for the gospel into their lives. The more such relationships we have, the greater is the inroad God can make through our lives. The composite *OIKOS* of a church-planting team makes up the potential church. Neighbour summarizes the problem of church-planting dysfunction when he states: 'Less than 1% of the salaried *pillars of the church* were (sic) investing one hour a week developing personal relationships with the huge mass of totally unchurched.'[13] Is Neighbour perhaps telling us that being off-the-job is really being on-the-job? Jesus

---

12 *Oikos* literally means 'household': the extended family plus slaves, which formed the basic agricultural and socio-economic unit in Ancient Greece.
13 Neighbour, p 82. Tom Wolf and Ralph Neighbour have illuminated the concept of *oikos* as it relates to evangelism.

taught us to be externally oriented, the focus upon which a good to great church-planting movement thrives. The future of every visible ministry is in the harvest (Matthew 9:35–38) – from there tomorrow's leaders will come. The future of the church is those people who, today, are not yet believers. The external mindset is the missional mindset.

Multiplication coordinator

Why is it that the challenge of church-planting multiplication in Europe hasn't yet been met? One reason lies in the energy and attention needed in planting just *one* church. Those of us who have planted churches, know of how depleting the task is. There is seldom energy left for other undertakings. Thus church planting gets accomplished at the expense of multiplication.

For church-planting multiplication to occur we need bi-focal vision. When we focus on the planting of one church, we can become 'near-sighted', unless we continue to be reminded of the 'far-sighted' vision, beyond the one new church to a plethora of new churches. Church planting with far-sighted vision leads to multiplication. This is where the church-planting coordinator comes into play. His job is to shepherd the process of multiplication, to look away from the immediate situation towards the horizon and beyond. He keeps far-sighted vision alive; he is the coach with the game plan, the air-traffic controller who anticipates all the flight paths before the planes take off or land.

The multiplication coordinator sees to it that the church plant is on track in terms of disciples made, leaders developed, coaches trained and teams generated for new churches to be launched. He functions as a midwife who guides the birth of a whole new generation of churches. The multiplication coordinator is also the 'genealogist' who can show us how an entire movement came into being and how its members are related.

Reproducible models

Every great movement needs healthy systems of reproduction that are better than the people using them. Such systems are not just practical, easy to use and reproductive, but they exert benevolent power upon their users. Benevolent power is the power to change into Christ-likeness and the power to reach outsiders.

In the church that we planted in the city of Kaiserslautern (pop. 100,000) we experimented with a hybrid form of triads.[14] The model is as simple as it is reproducible. Initially, three men or three women, all Christ-followers, band together to form a triad, or a mini-group. At the first meeting, an 'expiration date' of six months is given to the group. (Healthy mini-groups have this in common with yoghurt: both have an expiration date. The expiration date tells us how long we may count on their goodness.) Each member covenants together to exercise what Cole calls 'spiritual breathing'. In our context we each inhale (read) three chapters of God's word daily, all reading the same text. When we come together once a week we share how God has been speaking to us, and then we exhale (confess) how we have lived during the previous week. Much discipleship falls short of life change because it tells people how they *ought* to live. Only when we honestly tell one another how we *actually* live does deep life change occur. Thus we ask questions related to temptation, finances, family, anger and so on. In the process of the next several months we add a fourth member to the group.

At the end of the six months, each group meets for a meal to celebrate God's goodness and to signal the division of the group into two groups of two. Each dyad then invites a non-Christian from their OIKOS to join their mini-group for an initial two-week period. In this way we give the seeker enough time to get wooed by the grace of God as well as giving a convenient and face-saving exit, should he desire to discontinue. The groups are intent upon seeing non-Christians come to faith in Christ and continue on in life transformation in the mini-groups. These are again time-released to divide after six months.

The beauty of this reproducible system of disciple making is that it functions leaderlessly – it is not dependent upon giftedness to make it work. And it not only sees the lives of believers grow in spiritual depth; it is harvest-oriented – drawing new people into the kingdom of God by appropriating its essence for themselves.

'Grace is opposed to earning, but not to effort', says Dallas Willard.[15] It takes effort and a good reproducible model to make disciples. John Wesley discovered this in his reproducible system, which he labelled the

---

14 Made popular by Neil Cole. See Bibliography.
15 Willard, *The Great Omission*, pp 34, 61, 80.

'class meeting'. 'They met weekly to give an account of their personal spiritual growth, according to the rules and following the procedures which Wesley had carefully crafted.'[16] Life change occurs where there is nearness, openness, and accountability – the basis for movements of God that lead to healthy multiplication.

The Disciplines of a Church-Planting Multiplication Movement

If we look with Jesus at the end goal, we see the multiplication of churches. If we want to see this not only in our mind's eye but also in reality, in our day, we have to challenge our behaviour. A church-planting multiplication movement needs new disciplines.

Progressive vision

It is hard work to plant a new church. It will take all of our energy to ensure that everything works smoothly and stays on course. A new church plant can tend to create shortsightedness. Therefore a new discipline is needed: progressive vision. Despite the many tasks that are immediately before us, we dare not lose sight of what's ahead: the next church plant. Having 'progressive lenses' will enable us to keep a newly started ministry on course while at the same time never losing sight of the fact that the start of the next new congregation is just around the corner.

Multiplication of leaders

To do the ministry well is no longer enough. Of course we are expected to do the ministry well, whether preaching or teaching or serving others. But if we do not reproduce our ability to do these ministries, we will stagnate or burn out. One person alone will never have the power that a church-planting movement requires. In order to experience rapid multiplication, concentrate your efforts on the empowerment of new leaders who, in turn, are able to start new churches.

---

16 Henderson, p 11.

Church-wide missional exercises

In order to make the shift from addition to multiplication when it comes to church planting, we must move from evangelistic to missional activity. If we do, we will reach an increasing number of people for Christ. There are important differences between these two approaches: an evangelistic approach is focussed on the lost who need the gospel, who come to Christ, and who join the church. The emphasis is on communication of the gospel through speaking. By contrast, missionally-minded Christians seek to infiltrate society and its cultural sub-groups in order to be Christians among them where they are, in their milieu. A handful of disciples, called to reach a specific sociological group of non-Christians, lives among them as a shining light pointing to Christ. Seekers who become Christians stay in their environment and establish new groups in the old setting.

Vision casting

Because vision for the task God has entrusted to us grows dimmer, month-by-month, leaders of church-planting movements should constantly envision their people. Helping and leading them by example – talk about it, hear it, see it, witness it and celebrate it – this is the on-going task of those who lead a multiplication movement.

Prayer and Sabbath

In order to experience a fresh working of God, we have to raise our spiritual temperature. Not until the believers were united in faith-filled prayer was the world shaken (Acts 4:31; 12:5–17). When our churches learn to submerge themselves in prayer, they will live among the lost of their society with authority and power. An aspect of this is the discipline of keeping the Sabbath, in which we learn to rid ourselves of those things on which we are dependent. Instead, we depend completely on God. God does his best work when his children regularly disengage from their ministries and allow him to work.

The multiplication coordinator

For a multiplication movement to soar, a gifted leader is needed, one whose only job is to keep the church(es) on course to reproduce and multiply. This person will point out where God is at work. He will support the ministries that can contribute to multiplication. He will always keep in mind the six characteristics of a ministry of multiplication, and he will help the other leaders overcome obstacles. Without such a coordinator, leaders will be overwhelmed by the tension that arises between the here and now and the future that is ahead.

Problems that Occur with Multiplication

Certain problems can kill a movement before it has a chance to really get started. What follows is a description of six typical problems.

Short-sighted ministry

Short-sighted ministry concentrates on itself and its own efforts. It sees those it is currently reaching but lacks vision and energy to go beyond that.

Change of pastor or leadership change

Any time there is a change of leaders, there is always the danger that the new leadership will not embrace the vision of the previous leader.

Economic crisis

In times of recession, many people lose their employment. Others find it necessary to move to another city and therefore to another church. This can lead to a loss of volunteers, so that churches struggle to survive and stop nurturing the vision of expansion and multiplication.

Christian consumers

A multiplication movement is no place for comfortable 'couch-potato' Christians who simply want to sit and soak it all in. A real danger emerges when members expect the leaders to serve them – 'After all, that's what they're paid for.' In fact, the leaders should be teaching the members to assume responsibility for the various ministries and areas of service in order to build the kingdom of God.

Resistance within the denomination

A church-planting movement will die if it is important to maintain the status quo, whether in the local church or in a denomination. The multiplication of new churches tends to change the thinking and behaviour of an entire denomination. If the denominational leadership sees this as a threat, it may seek to stop the growing movement in its tracks.

Moral failure

Unfortunately it happens again and again: highly gifted men and women fall to a variety of temptations. Some of these leaders have to leave the ministry because of their failure, and their departure can mean the death of vision and of the entire movement.

At Pentecost, 3000 people came to faith in Christ on a single day and the first church was born. Missiologists calculate that all over our planet today, 3000 people are converted every day. In one of the few growing denominations in Germany, three people come to faith each day and become members of a local church.[17] We can be thankful for that but certainly not satisfied.

Although the Western world has experienced a new wave of church planting, many of these efforts remain at best in the category of 'addition'. It will take the power of God and the conscious, unyielding determination of men and women who have a deep longing to experience the birth of a magnificent church-planting movement.

The power of God and the power of determination make all the difference in the kinds of results we will see from our church-planting efforts. Our determination to rise above mediocrity and to achieve the exceptional will make a difference. We must determine to be goal-oriented, to be externally focussed and to reproduce ourselves if we truly want to see 'G7'-type churches established: churches that plant churches not by addition but by multiplication. As the missionary elder-statesman Roland

---

17 Statistical information from the Bund Freier evangelischer Gemeinden K.d.ö.R. (German Evangelical Free Church), from the years 2006–07. For UK information during the same time, see (all live in February 2013): http://www.whychurch.org.uk/denomination.php Further information for the UK available at: http://www.brin.ac.uk and also at: http://www.dur.ac.uk/churchgrowth.research/

Allen stated so poignantly: 'The really fantastic things of God lie beyond our control.'[18] Yes, the fantastic things that God does are beyond our control – but not beyond our faith or our influence. We must align ourselves with his word and cooperate with the Holy Spirit. The best church-planting endeavours are those that choose the road 'less traveled by'[19] which will change the destiny of countless numbers of people.

18 Allen, p 13.
19 After a phrase from the poem 'The Road Not Taken', by Robert Frost.

Afterword

The Glory of Jesus Christ and the Planting of New Churches

If you have read thus far, you belong to those who hunger to see new churches established. Why do Christians start new Christian churches? There are many (valid) answers to this question: because people without Christ are lost; in obedience to the Great Commission; as a response to evangelistic preaching; in order to reach more people for Jesus; to make God's kingdom visible. There is validity in each of these reasons.

Yet the loveliest and most important reason of all for starting new churches is to glorify Jesus Christ. Jesus asked his Father in heaven to allow his disciples to see his glory: 'Father, I desire that those also, whom you have given me, may be with me where I am, *to see my glory*, which you have given me because you loved me before the foundation of the world' (John 17:24, NRSV, Anglicized, author's emphasis). The theologian John Owen commented on this text: 'No man will ever see the glory of Christ in eternity who hasn't by faith already seen it in some measure in this world.'[1] Those doing the work of church planting are helping people to encounter Jesus, so that their eyes may be opened to see *his* glory, and that they may rejoice, both in this world and in eternity.

Unbelief is an expression of the inability to recognize the glory of God. People who do not believe in Christ see him as *Ichabod* (literally, 'the glory is departed'; 1 Samuel 4:21). They see in Jesus someone whose appearance

---

1 John Owen, *The Glory of Christ* (Chicago: Moody Press, 1980) pp 128–29.

is unattractive (Isaiah 53:2). For our contemporaries living in darkness a crucified Christ is either foolish or he is offensive – anything but glorious.

But isn't our God glorious?! His holiness and his humility are incomparable. Because no one could possibly work her way up to God, God sends himself down to us in Jesus. Because no one can ever remove his own guilt, Jesus takes upon himself all our sins and removes them from us. Because no one can justify herself before God, God gives us his own righteousness in Christ Jesus. Because we can never in our own strength live lives that are pleasing to God, God gives us his Holy Spirit, who becomes our joy and strength, for he enables us to do God's will. This is nothing less than glorious!

When we plant new churches, we glorify Jesus: we make him large, important, and valuable in the eyes of others. How is glory measured? A clear indication of the measure of Jesus' glory in a church is the joy that the members have: the greater their joy, the more they glorify Jesus.[2] How do we find this joy that glorifies Jesus? By looking at him and his works: 'And all of us, with unveiled faces, are seeing the glory of the Lord' (2 Corinthians 3:18, NRSV, Anglicized). Church planters are leaders who invite others to look and see Jesus in his beauty. By looking at Jesus in his glory, something surprising happens to us: '[we] are being transformed into the same image from one degree of glory to another' (2 Corinthians 3:18, NRSV, Anglicized). People are converted by the work of the Holy Spirit. After conversion, they find, through the Spirit, the freedom to do God's will – an inner change occurs through the Spirit (2 Corinthians 3:17–18). Christ's character 'bleeds' into the life of his children – we call that transformation – and his children reflect more and more of the glory of their Lord. The effect on the watching world is magnetic.

We refuse to plant churches where Jesus Christ is not the centre. We only want to plant churches where Jesus is glorified and the joy of the Lord is palpable and life-changing. The result is more glory for the One who gives life to the church, from both believers and non-believers. When a newly established church is radiant, people will 'see your good works and

---

2 This is a central theme in the writing of theologian John Piper and is also a fundamental truth of the Bible.

give glory to your Father in heaven' (Matthew 5:16). Jesus Christ is Lord and is glorified through a newly planted church.

I don't know about you, but I want to live my life in such a way that at the end of it I can say, 'I have no regrets'. What people regret at the end of their lives are all the things that have no eternal value. If you see that your purpose in life is to plant a church with Jesus as its essence, with his enabling your efforts, you will not only find joy but will also unleash joy among others. Planting new churches glorifies Jesus now and for all eternity.

I wish you God's blessing!

Dietrich Schindler

APPENDICES

Checklists for a
Church-Planting Project

Phase 1 Checklist – Build a Start-Up Team
Timeframe: 5–6 months

Start date: _____

The church planter and coach place a check mark by each item when it is accomplished:

____A minimum of 15–25 committed adults for the start-up team

____A coach assigned to the church planter

____Leaders build a network of relationships to 50–100 people

____The nature of a New Testament church studied and understood

____Clear, compelling profile developed (vision, values, goals)

____Undisputed leader of the project is known to all and has everyone's support

____Prayer team assembled and regularly supplied with prayer requests

____Vision nights conducted to reach interested Christians

____Assimilation activities begun (once or twice monthly)

____New people added to the start-up team

____Robust prayer life evident in team

_____Forward momentum is clearly evident

_____Introductory conversations held with area pastors, ministerial association, etc.

Accomplished on_____

If you have not met these criteria, your coach must be convinced that you may still proceed to the next phase notwithstanding.

Note: After each phase the church planter does the following tasks with the start-up team:

- Evaluation: What went well? What needs improvement?
- Consultation: How does the coach assess our progress?
- Celebration: Give God the glory, and express gratitude and recognition to the team and volunteers.

Phase 2 Checklist – Start Preview Worship Services
Timeframe: 6–12 months

Start date: _____

The church planter and coach place a check mark by each item when it is accomplished:

____Volunteers from the sending church (if there is one) provide support (music, technology, children's ministry, food)

____40–60 adults attend preview worship services

____10 new visitors from the local community attend each preview worship service

____Prolific word of mouth advertising results in many personal invitations being extended

____15–20 new people have been added to the start-up team

____Attractive facility (rented), bookkeeping and accountable financial system in place, regular donations received for the project

____Plan and find leaders for the five most essential areas: missional presence (being with non-Christians where they are), worship services, children, assimilation of new people, small groups

Accomplished on_____

If you have not met these criteria, your coach must be convinced that you may still proceed to the next phase notwithstanding.

Note: After each phase the church planter does the following things with the start-up team:

- Evaluation: What went well? What needs improvement?
- Consultation: How does the coach assess our progress?
- Celebration: Give God the glory, and express gratitude and recognition to the team and volunteers.

Phase 3 Checklist – Intensification
Timeframe: 6–9 months

Start date: _____

The church planter and coach place a check mark by each item when it is accomplished:

___Worship service attendance between 60–100 adults

___Half of the attenders participate in a small group

___Plan and carry out evangelistic events or culturally-relevant serving activities

___Worship services twice monthly

___Growing attendance at worship services

___Membership class designed to facilitate strong, committed members

___Special service celebrating the first members

Accomplished on_____

If you have not met these criteria, your coach must be convinced that you may still proceed to the next phase notwithstanding.

Note: After each phase the church planter does the following things with the start-up team:

- Evaluation: What went well? What needs improvement?
- Consultation: How does the coach assess our progress?
- Celebration: Give God the glory, and express gratitude and recognition to the team and volunteers.

Phase 4 Checklist – The Grand Opening
Timeframe: 4 weeks

Start date: _____

The church planter and coach place a check mark by each item when it is accomplished:

____Strong advertising campaign conducted

____Attractive, functional building leased for the occasion

____Leadership team established of mature Christ-followers who have leadership gifts, precursor to eldership

____New small groups created with new people (except the leaders)

____Vision and values are constantly discussed

____High quality printed material produced (introductory packet, church profile, sermon outlines, etc.)

Accomplished on_____

Note: After each phase the church planter does the following things with the start-up team:

- Evaluation: What went well? What needs improvement?
- Consultation: How does the coach assess our progress?
- Celebration: Give God the glory, and express gratitude and recognition to the team and volunteers.

APPENDIX B

Checklists for Church Planters Once the Church is Established

Carl George describes four growth stages in the life of a church planter:[1]

- Stage 1: Pastor as 'catalyzer' – he draws people in and motivates them
- Stage 2: Pastor as 'organizer' – when the church grows, he creates structures. He trains others and does less and less direct ministry himself
- Stage 3: Pastor as 'operator' – he delegates increasingly more ministries and oversees numerous ministry teams
- Stage 4: Pastor as 'redeveloper' – he continuously evaluates, eliminates what is ineffective, reorganizes, so that the church moves forward purposefully

Leaders *must* be able to 'morph' in order to lead the church to further growth. They must be able to change as the church grows so as not to become a bottleneck that hinders further development. Whereas leaders must do almost everything themselves in the beginning, they must learn to delegate with time. If they have led their team and volunteers well, they will increasingly assume oversight (care, shepherding) for ministry-area leaders rather than for individual volunteers.

---

1 Shenk & Stutzman, pp 176–78.

Beginning Phase Checklist – Stabilization
12–18 months after start-up

Start Date: _____

The church planter and coach place a check mark by each item when it is accomplished:

_____After prayer and consultation, put yearly goals in writing and communicate to the members

_____Volunteers meet regularly for prayer, discussion, and training

_____Small group leaders identify co-leaders, and groups experience healthy division to form new groups

_____Coaching system for leaders introduced

_____Church business meetings for members occur

_____Vision and values constantly talked about

_____Disciples are won and trained

_____Prayer is a strong element in the ethos of the church

Accomplished on_____

Note: After each stage, the church planter does the following things with the start-up team:

- Evaluation: What went well? What needs improvement?
- Consultation: How does the coach assess our progress?
- Celebration: Give God the glory, and express gratitude and recognition to the team and volunteers.

Expansion Phase Checklist
24–36 months after start-up

Start Date: _____

The church planter and coach place check mark by each item when it is accomplished:

_____Prayer is intensified

_____Ministry leaders are established for the various ministry areas

_____New ministries have been started

_____Ministries that have run their course have been eliminated

_____The church members live their lives incarnationally in various settings in the city

_____Leaders practice Sabbath rest and spiritual disciplines

_____Courage to practice church discipline (to rule out the unruly)

_____Elders are chosen

_____Coaching in place for all leaders and volunteers

Accomplished on_____

Note: After each phase in church planting, and on a half-yearly basis in all the minstry teams, leaders will do the following with their teams:

- Evaluation: What went well? What needs improvement?
- Consultation: How does the coach assess our progress?
- Celebration: Give God the glory, and express gratitude and recognition to the team and volunteers.

Multiplication Phase Checklist
36–60 months after start-up

Start Date: _____

The church planter and coach place a check mark by each item when it
is accomplished:

_____Ministry-area leaders have identified new leaders and reproduced
themselves

_____Prayer is the congregation's oxygen

_____Discipleship training is happening

_____Larger facilities have been obtained

_____The quality of the worship services has been improved by inviting
the help of an outside mentor with specialist gifts in this area

_____The vision for a new church-planting project grows stronger within
the leadership

_____Experienced leaders are authorized by the church leadership to start
a daughter church

_____The start-up team is commissioned and blessed by the sending
church to begin a new church plant

Accomplished on_____

To win more people for Christ requires more churches that have an outward orientation. In order for them to be able to reproduce, they must have
a healthy inner life, consisting primarily of disciples who make disciples
who, in turn, make disciples. Only people who have proven themselves
in this way are invited to coaches' training. Those who complete coaches'
training form a pool from which ministry-area leaders can be appointed,
and from them in turn, new church-planting teams will be formed.

The task is enormous, but so are the needs of millions of people who
are inching closer to a Christless eternity every day. There are great risks
involved. But the risk of doing nothing is far greater. The costs are high

– emotionally and physically. Yet each of us has but one life to live. Let us then resolve to live that life without regrets. The benefits are amazing: who can measure the worth of redeemed lives, standing side by side with church planters in eternity, church planters who have dared to trust Jesus for the enormous task of church planting and have seen it happen! *Carpe diem.* Seize the day, in the name of Jesus Christ!

APPENDIX C

Checklist for Disciples and Disciple Making

The following are goals in our life-long learning as disciples of Jesus. It is the goals a coach aims to encourage in those she coaches; and it is the goals each Christ-follower aims to encourage in the disciples he mentors.

	Spiritual Disciplines	Character	Competence
1	Quiet time	Love for God	Assurance of salvation
2	Repentance	Love for people	Bible study
3	Serving	Obedience	Victory over sin
4	Giving	Conscientiousness	Corporate prayer
5	Fasting	Commitment	Oikos friendships
6	Meditation	Humility	Active listening
7	Silence and solitude	Honesty	Personal witnessing
8	Prayer	Compassion	Explaining the gospel
9	Scripture memory	Self-control	Spiritual journal
10	Keeping in step with the Holy Spirit	Patience	Coaching
11		Kindness	Delegating
12		Generosity	Problem solving
13		Gentleness	Leading small groups

For each area, find appropriate tools that can help produce these traits that are:

- Easy to understand
- Easy to apply
- Easy to measure
- Easy to reproduce

Remember: First things first! One thing at a time! Only one additional task!

The Transformation Flow Chart

Ephesians 4:13 encourages us to grow into mature Christians. This is a checklist for mentoring personal spiritual transformation.

Name:_____ Date:_____

Prayer

How are you doing? Notes:	What has God been saying to you in your Bible reading? Notes:
What growth do you see in your walk with God? Notes:	Read Heb 12:1–2. (What must be discarded?) What must you yourself 'throw off'? Notes:
Read Acts 1:8 (What relationships are you building?) How are you yourself trying to reach non-Christians for Christ? Notes:	What does Jesus want to change in you? Notes:
What steps will you take before our next conversation? Notes: SMART goals	How can I pray for you? Notes:

Prayer

Done   Areas that need work: Next Bible reading:

○ _____

○ _____   Next appointment:

APPENDIX E

Lectio Divina

Lectio Divina is an ancient spiritual practice, found in the Early Church. *Lectio Divina* means the meditative, spiritual reading of God's word. In reading the Bible this way, we don't 'read' Scripture, but Scripture 'reads' us; we accept the invitation of the text and allow it to shape us. There are many examples in the Bible of God's word being used like this: Proverbs 4:3–4; Psalm 1:2; Luke 2:19, 51.

Practice: Participants are divided into groups of three.

Suggested text: John 15:1–8

Lectio Divina begins with an opening prayer that helps the participants to enter the presence of God and become aware that he is near. *Lectio Divina* consists of four parts, during which the same text is read four times. It is important to give participants ample time for silence, meditation and response after each reading.

Lectio: Read, so that God's word can be heard and digested.

Meditatio: Reflect upon a phrase, a part of a sentence or a single word that speaks to the heart. Why does this word/phrase touch me so deeply? What is it calling me to? In the group each participant briefly identifies his or her particular word or phrase.

Oratio: Respond with our own words. God has spoken to us and we respond with a desire to live accordingly.

Contemplatio: Allow the sweetness of this personal word from God to wash over the soul.

Tip: For the rest of the day, pray this personal word from God 'without ceasing'.

Bibliography

Allen, Roland. *The Spontaneous Expansion of the Church*. Eugene, OR: Wif and Stock Publishers, 1997.

Allen, Roland. *Missionary Methods: St. Paul's or Ours?* Grand Rapids: 1962.

Bonhoeffer, Dietrich. *Gemeinsames Leben*, 21ˢᵗ Edition. [English title: *Life Together*]. Munich: Kaiser, 1986.

Brooks, Phillips. *Lectures on Preaching*. Grand Rapids: Baker, 1969.

Cole, Neil. *Organische Gemeinde*. [English title: *Organic Church: Growing Faith Where Life Happens*]. Bruchsal: Gloryworld-Medien, 2008.

Collins, Gary R. *Christian Coaching: Helping Others Turn Potential into Reality*. Colorado Springs: Navpress, 2001.

DISG Persönlichkeitsprofil. Giengen, 1984 [English title: Sandy Kulkin, *The DISC Personality System: Enhance Communication and Relationships*].

Engel, James F. and Norton, H. Wilbert. *What's Gone Wrong with the Harvest? A Communication Strategy for the Church and World Evangelism*. Grand Rapids: Zondervan, 1975.

Foster, Richard J. *Nachfolge feiern: Geistliche Übungen neu entdeckt* [English title: *Celebration of Discipline: The Path to Spiritual Growth*]. Witten: SCM R.Brockhaus, 2010.

Gladwell, Malcolm. *The Tipping Point: How Little Things Can Make a Big Difference*. New York: Little, Brown and Company, 2000.

Henderson, D. Michael. *John Wesley's Class Meetings: A Model for Making Disciples*. Nappanee, IN: Evangel Publishing House, 1997.

Herbst, Michael. *Und sie dreht sich doch: Wie sich die Kirche im 21. Jahrhundert ändern kann und muss* [English translation of the title: 'She's Still Treading Water: How the 21st-Century Church Can and Must Change']. Aßlar: Gerth Medien, 2001.

Hesselgrave, David J. *Planting Churches Cross-Culturally: A Guide for Home and Foreign Missions / Planting Churches Cross-Culturally: North America and Beyond*, 2nd Edition. Grand Rapids: Baker Book House, 1980 / 2000.

Hettinga, Jan David. *Follow Me: Experience the Loving Leadership of Jesus.* Colorado Springs: Navpress, 1996.

Hybels, Bill. *Aufbruch zur Stille: Von der Lebenskunst, Zeit für das Gebet zu haben* [English title: *Too Busy Not to Pray*]. Aßlar: Gerth Medien, 2009.

Hybels, Bill. *Bekehre nicht, lebe!* [English title: *Becoming a Contagious Christian*]. Wiesbaden: Projektion J, 1994.

Huntington, Samuel P. *The Clash of Civilizations and the Remaking of World Order.* New York: Simon and Schuster, 1996.

Jenkins, Philip. *The Next Christendom: The Coming of Global Christianity.* Oxford: OUP, 2002.

Keller, Timothy J. and Thompson, J. Allen. *Church Planter Manual.* New York: Reedmer Presbyterian Church, 2002.

Kinlaw, Dennis C. *Spitzenleistungen durch effizientes Teamwork* [English title: *Coaching for Commitment: Interpersonal Strategies for Obtaining Superior Performance from Individuals and Teams*]. Gabler Verlag, 1993.

Klein, Stark, Schwarz. *Minigruppen: Der Weg zur ganzheitlichen Nachfolge* [English translation of the title: 'Mini-Groups: The Path to Holistic Discipleship']. Würzburg: Edition ACTS, 2000.

Lencioni, Patrick. *Mein Traum-Team oder die Kunst, Menschen zu idealer Zusammenarbeit zu führen* [English title: *The Five Dysfunctions of a Team*]. Frankfurt: Campus, 2004.

Lewis, Clive S. *The Weight of Glory and other Addresses.* New York: HarperCollins, 2001.

Lewis, Clive S. *Der Silberne Sessel,* 4 Auflage [English title: *The Silver Chair*]. Brendow Verlag, 2005.

Logan, Robert E. and Carlton, Sherilyn. *Das Coaching 1x1: Basiswissen und Alltagstipp* [English title: *Coaching 101: Discover the Power of Coaching*]. Gießen: Brunnen Verlag, 2004.

Logan, Robert E. and George, Carl. *Das Geheimnis der Gemeindeleitung* [English title: *Leading and Managing Your Church*]. Wiesbaden: C & P Verlag, 1987.

Logan, Robert E. and Ogne, Steven L. *Der Gemeindegründungs-Werkzeugkaste* [English title: *Church Planter's Tool Box*]. Frankfurt: Edition ACTS, 1991.

Logan, Robert E. *Be Fruitful and Multiply: Embracing God's Heart for Church Multiplication.* St. Charles, IL: Church Smart Resources, 2006.

Maxwell, John C. *Das Maxwell-Konzept: Entwickeln Sie Ihre Führungsqualität* [English title: *Developing the Leader Within You*]. Wiley-VCH Verlag, 2009.

McNeill, Donald P.; Nouwen, Henri J.M.; Morrison, Douglas A. *Compassion: A Reflection of the Christian Life.* New York: Doubleday, 1983.

Melzer, Friso. *Unsere Sprache im Lichte der Christus-Offenbarung*, 2 Auflage [English translation of the title: 'Our Language in Light of the Revelation of Christ']. Tübingen: Mohr Siebeck, 1952.

Neighbour, Ralph W. Jr. *Where Do We Go from Here? A Guidebook for Cell Group Churches*. Houston, TX: Touch Publications, 1990.

Nouwen, Henry J.M. *In the Name of Jesus: Reflections on Christian Leadership*. New York: The Crossroad Publishing Company, 1989.

Ogden, Greg. *Transforming Discipleship: Making Disciples a Few at a Time*. Downers Grove, IL: InterVarsity Press, 2003.

Ott, Craig. *Das Trainingsprogamm für Mitarbeiter: Biblische Grundsätze, Didaktische Hinweise, Praktische Modelle* [English translation of the title: 'Training Program for Volunteers: Didactic Instructions, Practical Models']. Gießen: Brunnen Verlag, 1996.

Phillips, J.B. *Your God Is Too Small*. New York: Simon and Schuster, 1997.

Reimer, Johannes. *Die Welt umarmen: Theologie des gesellschaftsrelevanten Gemeindebaus* [English translation of the title: 'Embrace the World: A Theology of Culturally Relevant Church Planting']. Marburg: Francke, 2009.

Robinson, Haddon W. *Biblical Preaching: The Development and Delivery of Expository Messages*. Grand Rapids, MI: Baker Book House, 1980.

Rust, Heinrich Christian. *Relevante Gemeinde* [English translation of the title: 'Relevant Church']. Kassel: Onken Verlag, 2009.

Schneider, Gerhard. 'Die Apostelgeschichte, Zweiter Teil (9:1–28:31)', *Herders Theologischer Kommentar zum Neuen Testament* [English translation of the title: 'Acts, Part 2', *Herder's Theological Commentary on the New Testament*]. Freiburg: Herder, 2002.

Schreyögg, Astrid. *Coaching: Eine Einführung für Praxis und Ausbildung* [English translation of the title: 'Coaching: An Introduction for Praxis and Training']. Frankfurt a.M.: Campus, 1995.

Schwarz, Christian A. *Die natürliche Gemeindeentwicklung* [English translation of the title: 'Natural Church Development']. Wiesbaden: C & P Verlag, 1996.

Shenk, David W. and Stutzman, Ervin R. *Creating Communities of the Kingdom: New Testament Models of Church Planting*. Scottdale, PA: Herald Press, 1988.

Stott, John R.W. *Between Two Worlds: The Art of Preaching in the Twentieth Century*. Grand Rapids: Eerdmans, 1982.

Thielicke, Helmut. *Theologische Ethik*, Volume 1, 5th Edition [English title: *Theological Ethics*]. Tübingen: J.C.B. Mohr, 1981.

Wagner, C. Peter. *Eine wachsende Gemeinde leiten* [English title: *Your Spiritual Gifts can Help your Church Grow*]. Lörrach: Wolfgang Simson Verlag, 1991.

Whitmore, John. *Coaching for Performance*, 3rd edition. London: Nicholas Brealey Publishing, 2002.

Willard, Dallas. *The Spirit of the Disciplines: Understanding How God Changes Lives*. HarperSanFrancisco, 1991.

Willard, Dallas. *Renovation of the Heart: Putting on the Character of Christ*. Colorado Springs: Navpress, 2002.

Willard, Dallas. *The Great Omission: Reclaiming Jesus's Essential Teachings on Discipleship*. San Francisco: HarperCollins, 2006.

CPSIA information can be obtained at www.ICGtesting.com
Printed in the USA
BVOW03s0848060214

344021BV00009B/259/P